Pivotal points to success shared by RISE Collaborative members

ON THE RISE

VOLUME 2

Stacy Taubman and Kate Wiegmann

On the RISE, Volume 2

Pivotal points to success shared by members of RISE Collaborative Workspace

Stacy Taubman and Kate Wiegmann
On the RISE Press

Published by On the RISE Press, St. Louis, MO
Copyright ©2018 Stacy Taubman and Kate Wiegmann
All rights reserved.

Editor: Catherine Mros

Cover and Interior design: Jen Seris, www.jenseris.com

Project management: Kate Wiegmann and Abby Mros

Library of Congress Cataloging-in-Publication Data

Library of Congress Control Number: 2018912882

Stacy Taubman and Kate Wiegmann

On the RISE, Volume 2: Pivotal points to success shared by members of RISE Collaborative Workspace

ISBN: 978-0-9997525-2-4

Library of Congress subject headings:

1. BUS109000: Business & Economics/Women in Business 2. SEL027000: Self-Help/Personal Growth/Success 3. BUS025000: Business & Economics/ Entrepreneurship

This book is dedicated to the times

we fall down and the times we rise.

To the mistakes we make and the lessons we learn.

To the doubters and the cheerleaders.

To the fears and the dreams.

We wouldn't be here without all of them, so thank you.

"There is no force more powerful

than a woman determined to rise."

Bosa Sebele

Contents

Epigraph 5
Bosa Sebele

Introduction 9
Stacy Taubman and Kate Wiegmann

The Real Story 11
Stacy Taubman

The Truth About the Lies We Tell Ourselves 19
Allison Schaper

Dirty Laundry 27
Jean Scholtes

Still Standing 35
Adrian E. Bracy

On the Right Track 43
Ria Ruthsatz

Tick of the Clock 51
Erin Warner Prange

The Serial Achiever 59
Kerri Mileski

Gratitude 67
Ladan Kamfar

Wake Up Call 75
Heather J. Crider

The Chicken Incident 83
Joy Roberts

Passing the Torch: Mentors & Professional Success 93
Amy Hoch Hogenson

Out of the Ashes 101
Holly Cunningham

It's a Millennial! 109
Lynne Hayes

Redefining Success 117
Johnna Beckham

How Did I Get Here? 125
Julie Jones

Stay Safe 133
Jessica Rask

Making the Call 143
Kate Kerr

In This Moment 153
Kate Wiegmann

Afterword 161
Abby Mros

Introduction

I n 2016, we opened RISE Collaborative in St. Louis as a place for professional women to find community and grow their businesses. It was admittedly a little selfish; we were craving that in our lives, and it turns out we weren't alone. Hundreds of St. Louis' most impressive, ambitious women have come to RISE Collaborative seeking and finding the same thing we needed: community, connections, and confidence.

Humans are wired to search for connection. We want to be seen by other people and be valued. And one of the most effective, yet challenging, ways to build authentic connections with others is by being vulnerable. All of the Brené Brown fans are nodding their heads in agreement right now, and if you have no idea what we're talking about, please stop reading and go get a copy of *Daring Greatly!*

There are few things more vulnerable than sharing with others your mistakes, feelings, or secrets. Even sharing how proud or empowered you feel isn't something many women are comfortable doing! But that's exactly what the authors in the first volume of our anthology did. They opened up and the results were powerful.

We knew (hoped!) that our first anthology would make readers feel heard, inspired, and motivated. And they were! But we didn't anticipate how deeply the writing process would touch the authors themselves. Going through the process of pushing yourself to achieve a personal goal is powerful. Opening yourself up through vulnerability while hitting that goal? That's next-level relationship building.

Volume 2 is no different. In the book you are about to read are stories of vulnerability, growth, success and failure, and rising with strength. Every chapter offers new insight into connection and inspiration, which will leave you energized and challenged to think about your own experiences and goals. These stories are unparalleled examples of women supporting women, leading in their fields, and coming out on top, even in the face of challenges and loss.

The women in this anthology broke past fear and shame to bear their truths for each other and for readers. In doing so, they connected. They are more connected to each other, to the RISE community, and to you. We hope you feel the vulnerability and strength in these pages and that these truths can help you release some of your own. Find your own community, connections, and confidence in these pages with us.

Stacy Taubman　　**Kate Wiegmann**
Founder/CEO　　*Partner/COO*

The Real Story

Stacy Taubman

My heart is pounding and I'm hiding out in my office (something I do more regularly than I care to admit). In 30 minutes I have to stand up in front of 300 people who came to celebrate RISE Collaborative's first year in business. As the founder/CEO, you would think I would feel incredibly excited and proud that so many people from the community came out to celebrate our success. While I am honored and grateful, the only emotion coursing through my body is anxiety. Surprisingly, I suffer from social anxiety and am often extremely nervous before public speaking.

The fact that the room is filled with familiar faces, members, friends, and supporters makes no difference to my anxiety. And despite my fear, I absolutely have to stand up in front of the crowd and share "wise" words as founder/CEO.

Simon Sinek's words are echoing in my head: "People care about the why, not the what." I'll put the "Cliff's Notes" version of how RISE began below, but you can find the full story in Volume 1 of this anthology series:

> *After teaching math for 12 years and collecting a Master's in School Administration and School Counseling, I was floundering and unsure what was next in my career. I ultimately decided to start a tutoring and coaching*

company for high school girls in January 2013, while still teaching full time. I had enough success out of the gate to give me the courage to leave education and make this my full-time job. What I took for granted, though, was how much my classroom and my peers were a big part of my success. After interviewing 300 women in the community, I realized they were craving the same things I was: the opportunity to give back to the next generation, the ability to connect with other women who are striving, and the flexibility of a coffee shop with the polish of a corner office. And so RISE Collaborative came to be...

While that story is absolutely true, I have since realized there is more to the story than that.

An analogy that is often applied to entrepreneurship is that of an iceberg. People only see the part that has surfaced, but 90 percent of its mass is actually underwater, hidden from the world at large. The same is true about my journey, and it turns out that this path began way before my teaching days. It actually began early in my childhood.

Growing up was tough for me. I grew up in the suburbs of St. Louis, Missouri in an area with quite a bit of "new money," something which we definitely didn't have. We weren't poor by any means, and we were fortunate to have food on the table. But at an age when kids are cruel and all you desperately want is to fit in, I was regularly made fun of for my bargain-brand clothing. It was made very clear to me that my lack of name-brand outfits somehow made me less acceptable in the social hierarchy of our school.

To make matters worse, I was one of the only Jewish kids at my school and faced antisemitism. Hearing slurs about being a "Jew" was not an uncommon experience for me. It didn't help that I started speaking late (my father says I've been making up for it ever since). When I finally did begin to communicate, I had quite the speech impediment. I couldn't pronounce my R's or S's and went to speech therapy throughout elementary school. For many years after, people often asked me if I was from New York because of how I pronounced my R's.

Let's add one more thing to the list: I was lucky enough to grow up in the 80s with huge and frizzy permed hair, Coke bottle glasses that took up much of my face, a mouth full of metal, and ears that stuck out. Let me tell you, not the best combination.

All of those things mixed into one package definitely didn't help my desperate desire to "fit in," and I spent most of my youth feeling like I wasn't good enough. I definitely faced bullying from the neighborhood kids and it was a very difficult time in my life.

The turning point for me was when I started gymnastics. I had always been the girl doing cartwheels and handstands in the outfield, and after watching the movie *Nadia*, I begged my parents to let me take gymnastics. From the moment I stepped into the gym, a feeling of "home" washed over me. I was hooked from day one and wanted to be there as much as humanly possible—no matter what! Once, I had a fever and my dad wanted to keep me home sick from practice. I accidentally broke our thermometer shaking it so hard to bring the temperature down so I could still go!

It was intoxicating to be in a space where my daily struggles at school fell by the wayside and I was surrounded by people who came from all walks of life striving for success. Finally I was with people who "got me" and I could stop bracing for impact from a cruel word or treatment from the kids at school

When I made the competitive team, my life improved even more. My confidence soared as I took the sport—and myself— more seriously. And I loved being a part of something bigger than myself, where it didn't matter where my clothes were from, what religion I was, how I spoke, or how I looked. I finally had authentic friendships with people who accepted me and shared a common interest. While we were all working on very different skills and it wasn't a team sport so to speak, I always knew where to look for a word of encouragement and support. Being on the gymnastics team gave me a sense of belonging that I so desperately needed. What a powerful feeling!

I recognize there are many out there who have had it much worse than I did, but elementary and middle school were definitely tough for me. I truly wonder how different my life would have ended up without gymnastics and the sense of belonging at such a formative age. Without having something

I was passionate about and a place where I felt at home, my life could have gone down a very different path. Gymnastics gave me the support network I needed and instilled a sense of confidence that helped propel me to where I am today.

Ever since I "retired" from gymnastics, I think I have been craving that same supportive environment, and starting a business in 2013 only amplified that feeling. I craved the feeling of being surrounded by people who are ambitious and striving. Instead of working alone in a coffee shop, I needed a place where I could let my "armor" down, be my authentic self, and not only be accepted, but celebrated.

Just like so many entrepreneurs have done before me, I decided to create a company that solved my problem since I couldn't find what I was craving. It took many years, many mistakes, and many people coming to the table to make it happen, but we finally opened our doors in early 2017, and I am proud of the community we have created. It is a place where professional women from different walks of life, career paths, and ages can feel "at home" just like I did in gymnastics. While our members work in different industries and may have very different goals from one another, they are collectively striving for more. The same feeling of home washes over me every time I walk into RISE, and I love when I hear our members share that sentiment.

I wish I could tell you I bravely emerged from my office and eloquently delivered this message in a speech to the 300 people at our anniversary party. To be honest, most of what I actually said is a complete blur, but what isn't a blur is the love and support that filled the room that night.

Through RISE Collaborative, I am once again part of something bigger than myself; it's intoxicating and game-changing. Our community makes me believe we can and should open RISE Collaboratives all over the world to impact countless women's lives. Our members pick me up when I am utterly exhausted and feel like I can't possibly continue. They give me purpose in life and I am so incredibly honored that they want to be a part of this ride.

STACY TAUBMAN As the Founder/CEO of RISE Collaborative, Stacy Taubman launched a company that is changing the way women do business. RISE Collaborative Workspace has been featured in USA Today, Bloomberg, The Today Show, ELLE Magazine, The Denver Post, St. Louis Business Journal, and more as a leader in the multi-billion-dollar coworking industry. Since opening in St. Louis in early 2017, RISE Collaborative's growing membership includes more than 250 of the city's most impressive business women. A second location is set to open in Denver in early 2019. Focused on empowering women in business and building social capital, Stacy and RISE Collaborative create meaningful connections between individuals, companies and organizations to foster a stronger and healthier business community for women. Dozens of members have reported business growth of 200 percent or more since joining RISE

continued

Collaborative, a true testament to the impact investing in women can have.

Stacy is also a sought-after public speaker and thought leader, having moderated talks with businesswoman and fashion icon Nicole Miller, and sisters Jenna Bush Hager and Barbara Bush Coyne, among many others. She regularly speaks at conferences on female entrepreneurship, social capital, and women empowerment, and co-hosts a podcast, Women on the RISE.

Stacy Taubman

stacy@riseworkspace.com

RISEworkspace.com | facebook.com/RISECollaborativeWorkspace

instagram.com/RISECollaborativeWorkspace | twitter.com/RISEcollabwkspc | linkedin.com/in/stacytaubman

The Truth About The Lies We Tell Ourselves

Allison Schaper

I consider myself a successful, career-driven lawyer who juggles a family with always trying to push her career forward. This is a piece of my path. Although it hasn't been a traditional path—and definitely not one I chose or saw coming—it has been a surprising adventure. More importantly, it is a path that I now recognize was necessary to walk in order to overcome the lies I was telling myself—even if I wasn't aware of them. It has also sparked a passion in me to help other women who may be telling themselves the same lies.

Flashback to 2010, I'm sitting in the unemployment office. For the first time in my life, I wholeheartedly feel like a failure—and it feels like slowly drowning in a barrel of molasses. I look around and try to tell myself that I am different from all of the other people here. I am a college graduate—hell, a law school graduate! I was a Division I athlete and captain of my team. I am the hardest worker I know. Yet, I cannot help but feel like that's just my way of patting myself on the shoulder and saying, "Sure honey. We know." Because what difference does all of that make now? I am exactly like everyone else here. We all have skills, talents, and strengths. And we are all just trying to keep our weekly checks coming in.

I meet with the employee assigned with the task of making sure that I am, in fact, trying to get a job. I want to shout at her, "Do you think I want to keep coming in here? Of course I'm trying!" I manage to state the same sentiment with a, "Yes, of course I have been looking. Here is a list of all of my efforts." She offers helpful advice and tips such as, "We have a typing course if that's something you need help with." I politely tell her that I think my administrative skills are up to par and I eventually leave, pretty sure that we now both feel helpless and inadequate. *Lie #1. My past defines my future successes.*

Rinse. Repeat. A couple of months pass. Then one morning, I get a call from a temp agency about an attorney contract position that is available. They are staffing a case at a big fancy law firm downtown and I have been selected to be interviewed. This is it! They won't know what hit them when I sit down in that chair! So I put on the best—and only—suit I own and navigate my way to what I'm sure is my bright and shiny future. But I am ushered into a room full of countless other people wanting the same position. We are all given forms to fill out, and in the end...we are all selected. No interview. No interaction with anyone at the firm. We are all selected.

"Okay. So maybe not the most stringent of criteria," I think. Show up and get selected. But that's fine. I just need my chance to shine. And if all of these other people have been feeling as defeated as I have been, then good for them, too!

We are taken in groups to meet with the attorneys leading the case. They make a quick presentation to my group, give us some paperwork, and escort us to where we will be working.

I am so excited. This place is beautiful! I can only imagine what my new workspace will look like. We get on the elevator. Down. Down. Down. We eventually get off at some basement floor that is undergoing renovations. There is a sea of plastic folding tables and chairs arranged in long rows amidst bare columns and missing ceiling tiles. "Pick a spot and we'll make sure you can all get connected to the internet." I should have known. I have been trying to get a job at a firm like this for months. Did I really think I would just get a phone call and that would be it? *Lie #2. I am not smart enough. I am not qualified.*

This humbling experience goes on for a few more jobs. However, the disappointment lessens with each one as my expectations plummet. Then I get a call from the temp agency saying I have another interview. But something is different this time; there's only one position they're filling. So I put on my trusty ol' suit and head out. The interview goes well and I am selected. This feels different. I tell my husband, "I'm digging my claws into this place and they are not getting rid of me!" That mindset alone changed my path.

I had always performed my tasks skillfully and ahead of time. But this time, I am actively looking for ways to do more than what's asked. It should have seemed obvious, but when I was with large groups of people who were all doing just the task at hand, it seemed silly to try to go a different direction. It felt like submitting an additional book report for extra credit that no teacher approved or asked for. But now that I am on my own, it seems simple and second nature to innovate and create shortcuts, to organize data in a more meaningful way, and to begin spotting documents that could potentially be problematic in the future. ***Lie #3. Success is a finite commodity.***

My point of contact at the firm is the senior paralegal, Janine. As I am doing all of this extra work, I give her copies she can share with the team. In no time, she is asking for follow up. How did I make certain charts? Where was this information? The team is interested in my work! This is great! I later come to find out that Janine has been taking all of my work and presenting it to the attorneys as her own. All of that follow up was, in fact, from the attorneys asking her to update or expand upon "her work." Then she would come back to me and no one was the wiser.

Janine would go on to question my timesheets, call into question my honesty, and intentionally make me late to meetings. But I never forgot my declaration—I was digging my claws in and I was going to make someone see my value. I stop sending Janine my work and instead begin directly emailing the senior attorneys myself, including my ideas for possible next steps for them to consider. If I do not hear back, I begin moving forward on my ideas and seeing which ones pan out. I take meticulous notes on what I have done, when, and how many times. I no longer depend on having a buddy with me to walk to meetings or get lunch.

Then, one day, there is a turn of events. The attorneys I'm working with are moving firms, and because of the dedication I have shown, they ask me to come with them. My meticulous, hard work is finally paying off! "Count me in!" Janine does not come with us. ***Truth #1: I control my success.***

The new firm is a breath of fresh air. I feel like my soul is more cleansed every time I walk through the door. After some time, one of the firm's partners who is also on the board, Troy, invites me out to dinner with several of the firm's other partners. I tensely agree and remind myself not to speak too much so I don't embarrass myself. That plan falls flat on its face almost immediately when Troy turns and asks about my career before the server even puts the bread basket on the table.

So out with my story I go. It's hard for me to get a read on how they are receiving me—these are seasoned litigators after all—and the conversation quickly turns to current and potential clients. At the end of the dinner, I'm still not quite sure what sort of impression I made, but no one seemed to be mortified or offended.

Shortly thereafter, I have my mid-year review. And guess who is conducting it: Troy. Not having been through a review before, I'm not sure what to expect. But when I sit down, Troy wants to talk very little about my numbers and projections, which he assures me are all fine. No, he wants to talk about promoting me and putting me on the path to partnership! ***Truth #2. I am smart enough. I am qualified.***

The years since that day seem to both crawl and fly by depending on the day. I am still at the same firm, although I have a much different perspective of it now than from the first day. Sometimes I find myself in the position of speaking to fellow female attorneys who, although they have not had my same experience, have told themselves my same lies.

I serve on the firm's national and local Women's Initiative Committees. I try to share my story and experiences as honestly as possible if it seems like they will help someone else. But mostly, I try to encourage all women to see themselves in a better light. To know they are in command of their futures. They are smart enough to do whatever they want to do. I have never found that the promotion of another woman has negatively affected me. In fact, I've seen the complete opposite to be true: every speaking engagement a woman lands, award she wins, trial she completes, new client she signs lifts us all up, if only for a brief moment in the course of our bustling days. ***Truth #3. There is always enough success to go around.***

ALLISON SCHAPER is a commercial and environmental litigator at Polsinelli PC where she defends corporations in various contract, tort, personal injury, and environmental contamination disputes. She has experience both in the courtroom, and at arbitrations and mediations. She puts all she has into fighting for her clients while respecting the rule of law and exceeding the stringent ethical standards imposed on attorneys. Allison graduated with a degree in psychology from Miami of Ohio and attended the University of Dayton School of Law where she served on the Honor Committee performing investigations into ethical violations and rewriting the honor code.

Allison additionally has interests in softball, pit bull rescues, and the real estate and construction industries. The latter interests are fueled and fostered by her husband, Jeff, who is a Vice President of Benton Homebuilders and constant source of support and strength. Allison

continued

and Jeff have a four-year-old daughter who they cannot keep out of the water and an eight-year-old rescued pit bull that refuses to get her paws wet. In her non-existent free time, Allison enjoys boating with her family in the summers and gathering around bonfires in the winter.

Allison Schaper

aschaper@polsinelli.com

polsinelli.com/professionals/aschaper | linkedin.com/in/schaperallison

Dirty Laundry
Jean Scholtes

As the Founder of KIND soap company, I've worked hard to create a brand, build a business, and project an "effortlessly successful entrepreneur" persona to the world. But I'm going to come clean and be authentic to my real self: "unsure and struggling entrepreneur desperately trying to keep her head above water."

First, some background info: I started making natural bath and body products in my basement out of sheer desperation. I was on a mission to find an alternative to steroids for my four-year-old son's severe eczema. The products on the market were full of ingredients that only made things worse, and I was at my wit's end. Through trial and error I created a bar of oatmeal soap that worked wonders on my son. After only a month of using it, the eczema cleared up. I developed other personal care products in the same manner, with safe and natural ingredients. I saw incredible results in my own skin, and my family went from skeptic guinea pigs to enthusiastic evangelists, but it was the difference in my son that made me realize I needed to share what I had created.

I had spent my career as a Creative Director helping other people build their brands, so I decided to combine that experience with this new passion and create my own. After a couple years of side-hustle development, I went all-in in 2011. A big part of getting through those early years was my Aunt Jill. She believed in me when other people probably thought I was making a huge mistake. Not only did she work for me for free for several years, she and my uncle wrote a check that helped me get my first store open.

Since then, a lot has happened. I have grown from making products in my basement to selling them at Whole Foods. From a folding table at the farmer's market to a 1,000-square-foot brick-and-mortar store. From selling a product online every once in a while to shipping orders out all over the country every day. I've gone from doing everything myself to employing a team of amazing women to help me grow the business.

The KIND brand now has more than 100 products in five product categories. We have been growing more than 30 percent year over year. I've won awards; been interviewed on TV, radio, and podcasts; rubbed elbows with celebrities at the Emmys; and been featured in respected publications. I was selected from 500 applicants from 56 countries to be in one of the best business accelerator programs in the country. (I know I'm tooting my own horn so hard right now that I've got Louis Armstrong cheeks, but I'm hoping to eventually make a point.)

When I've been asked to tell my KIND story over the years, I've always left out the not-so-glamorous bits. The "dirty laundry," per se. I'm infinitely more comfortable playing the highlight reel. Who isn't? Well, I hope it's not calling for rain because I'm hanging the laundry out for the whole neighborhood to see—granny panties and all.

The reality is, things have never been anywhere close to "effortless." I have struggled with depression all of my adult life and in recent years have received the additional gift of anxiety. I have no doubt that if I was "normal" and working at 100 percent of my ability, I would be much farther along in my business than I am now. I estimate that I have averaged around 65 percent for the past eight years. So those accomplishments I listed? I have a hard time accepting praise or kudos for them. Like Shania Twain says, "They don't impress me much." I know where I could be. Where I should be.

I feel a lot of guilt and anxiety because of that. When the weight and fog of depression arrives, I want so badly to shake it off, to be "normal," but I just can't. I have days when simple tasks like showering or making a phone call seem insurmountable. Sometimes I feel like my body and mind aren't on the same page. My mind is full of ideas and plans but my body isn't receiving the transmission to get up and make them happen. I've had full blown anxiety attacks over business decisions where I thought I might need to call an ambulance because I felt like someone was crushing me from the inside out.

In my early twenties, I was blindsided when my doctor when suggested I may be depressed. I thought I was normal. How could I possibly be depressed? He had me fill out a sheet of about 30 questions while I was at his office with stomach pains and unexplainable fatigue (both symptoms of depression). I started the questionnaire 100-percent sure he was wrong and finished very confused by all of my checked boxes. It went something like:

1. Do you have trouble waking up in the morning after a full night's sleep? I'm a big sleeper. I love to sleep. No big deal. Check.

15. Do you have difficulty focusing, concentrating, or completing tasks? Say what? I need to read that again...I wonder if I have stuff to make spaghetti tonight?...Dang it!! Check.

30. Do you have trouble remembering names or sometimes struggle with recalling basic words? Oh, for the love of God. Yes, okay? Dr. What's-his-name over there is looking all smug, like he's so smart. Check.

Good news: I aced the test! Bad news: I aced the test...

Since I'm really going to air it all out and tell the whole story, I should probably add some of the other struggles that compounded my depression and anxiety significantly. The company my husband worked for closed around the same time I opened my store. The job market was abysmal, so he switched to start-up mode as well. We went more than a year without income or health insurance and used credit cards to put food on the table for our four kids and to finance the businesses. We eventually accumulated more than $100,000 in debt. There were times when our "regular" financial crisis went into "red alert" status, and we fought over who needed to go get a "real job" (or go live in a van down by the river).

Collection agencies inevitably came a-callin.' When they realized that there was no blood to get from our turnip, they started harassing my parents. I'll also throw in the proud moment of my car being repossessed while said parents were visiting. Oh, and our house was foreclosed on! But since the bank had so many houses in the same predicament at the time, we were somehow able to refinance and get back in the bank's good graces before they got to ours.

During these years, I was juggling medications with my doctor, trying to keep my head above water. I could only afford generic meds so my doc had his work cut out for him. Of course, therapy was recommended, but I couldn't afford it.

As if all of that wasn't enough of a challenge, in the middle of all this my dear Aunt Jill died. She was only 56. Her death hit me hard and sent me into a downward spiral. It took me a year to talk about her without crying. For a long time, I worried each time a customer came in that they would say, "Where's Jill? I haven't seen her in a while!" Not to mention, she had been doing most of the left-brain tasks in the business and had far surpassed my rudimentary knowledge of QuickBooks. Lucky for me, my friend with a fitting name, Angela (an angel), had just left her job at Panera and needed a little break from corporate America. She offered to help me out between jobs—but I never let her go. She's now our COO and keeps the business (and me) afloat and pointed in the right direction.

I expect that people who know me will read this chapter and be surprised. I do a pretty good job of masking my depression and anxiety. So why am I now sharing all of this with the world? Maybe it's because I'm at a point in my life where being truly authentic is more important than keeping up appearances. Or because I've reached an age where I care less about what people think of me and more about what people think of themselves. Mostly it's because sharing all of this might help someone see that nothing should stop them from working toward their goals in life. And that it's human nature to want to project an ideal version of ourselves to the world, but the reality is, no one is perfect and everyone has "laundry" of some sort to deal with.

I've come to realize that what I have struggled with isn't "dirty" laundry (it's not like I buried a collections agent out in the desert or anything), and I shouldn't be afraid, or ashamed to let people see it...even those granny panties blowing in the breeze. I'm not going to run out and yank them off the line anymore when the neighbor looks over the fence. I'm just going to say, "Good morning! Yep, they're mine!" They may not be sexy but dang it, they're comfortable, which is how I finally feel in my own skin.

JEAN SCHOLTES is the founder and Chief Executive Officer of KIND soap company. KIND is a line of natural bath, body and beauty products with a mission to be KIND to your skin, KIND to the earth, and KIND to others. It was her son's issues with eczema that prompted Jean to start creating her own products. She sought education in formulation and manufacturing at The American College of Healthcare Sciences in Portland, Oregon where she earned a Certificate in Aromatherapy. KIND products are available at their shop in Webster Groves, online, and at a variety of stores like Whole Foods and Soft Surroundings. Before founding KIND, Jean worked in advertising agencies designing packaging and building brands. Prior to that she was the Creative Director of Sara Lee for 10 years where she lead a team of designers and project managers and was responsible for the creation and production of all packaging, marketing, and promotional materials. Jean earned a Bachelor's degree in Visual Communications from Southern Illinois

continued

University at Carbondale in 1993 and began her career as a graphic designer for the Roadmaster Corporation designing bicycles. Jean and her husband, Jeff, have four teenagers (and two dogs!) that keep them very busy.

Jean Scholtes

jean@kindsoap.com

kindsoap.com | facebook.com/KINDsoap | instagram.com/kindsoap

ᗸ

Still Standing
Adrian E. Bracy

I may work with numbers, but adjectives have played an awfully large role in my life and career.

Female. First. Black.

These three words have brought me the greatest pride, strength, and drive imaginable. They've also been used against me.

"First Black female CFO in the NFL" is the one I'm best known for.

But these three adjectives guided and shaped my life and career in ways no one could have thought possible, least of all me.

After I was born, my biological mother was admitted to a mental institution. I never had the opportunity to really know her before her death.

Mental illness isn't something many women talk about in the Black community, but it is pervasive and important to discuss. It's not a part of my journey I've spoken much about before; in fact, I tend to leave out exactly what it was we lost my mother to and let others draw their own conclusions. But I've realized it had such a profound impact on me and I can possibly make a difference by bringing awareness to it. From my very earliest days, wanting to give a voice to the weak and helping those who need a hand up was a part of my being.

My great aunt raised me for 10 years, which was a gift to my mother and my future by giving me a female influence. And then another woman, Dorothy Brown—my cousin—raised and ultimately adopted me. Yet another gift and blessing for my future, which could have gotten lost in the shuffle of poverty, crime, and chaos that otherwise ruled Liberty City, the Miami neighborhood I was raised in.

But life wasn't easy; far from it. To keep up the façade of being middle class in school, I had to work cleaning houses and at a fast food restaurant in between my studies. But I'm convinced I was better for it. To know what it's like to want for things and then work hard for them.

My adoptive parents lived in a better school district, and for the first time, I was exposed to ambitious girls who wanted to be doctors and lawyers. Until that point, every woman I knew was a housekeeper, secretary, or restaurant worker so the idea that, as a woman, I could aspire to something else was life-changing.

I was determined to be the first in my family to go to college. In between work and my studies, I had become an accomplished track athlete, but decided to turn down a scholarship to a large Florida university to instead attend Morgan State University, a historically black college in Maryland.

Setting an unattainable goal and achieving it set in motion a career future with greater titles, opportunities, and accomplishments than I ever imagined. Yet these same three words continued to influence me in good ways and destructive ones.

Accounting and numbers became my forte. Perhaps it was the reliability of numbers that drew me in: something real, practical, and solvable where my past had been unpredictable.

Soon, being a woman became something significant in my career—a differentiating factor that punctuated my achievements. I was hired by male-dominated companies—aviation, manufacturing, and then football—where I was frequently one of or the only woman in the room.

It would be lovely to tell you that these companies embraced my role as a female leader and recognized the advantages that having a woman involved in key decisions would provide. And that I affected great organizational change and did so with strength and graceful leadership.

But that's not quite how it happened.

At the aviation company, I served as Controller and exceeded expectations. I led the department and did the lion's share of the work, but it was all worth it because I was respected and had what I thought was my dream job. Until one day new management took over and decided they wanted a CFO. While I had nearly all of the qualifications they were looking for, there was one I couldn't meet. He wanted a man in this leadership role.

Although I'm not big on titles and bureaucracy, there is something to be said about your title reflecting your contributions. When the new CFO was brought in, the only change that came was that he received the title, but I was doing all of his work. After all, he had no accounting experience, so how could he?! He was the figurehead and I dutifully played the amenable female who smiled, played nice, and kept her head down.

I cried in my car each morning as I prepared myself for the indignity and frustration of the day ahead. Like many women do, I wanted to set a good example for the rest of our staff, stay positive, and retain what I knew was a good, secure job. But I was sacrificing my sanity, was unappreciated, and quite frankly was discriminated against both as a woman and an African American.

Eventually, I gathered the strength and self-respect to leave. But that wouldn't be the last time I had to leave a job for my sanity.

In 1991, I took a job with the Miami Dolphins, which would begin an 18-year career in the NFL and some of the greatest accomplishments, lessons, and challenges in my career. I rose through the ranks of the financial department from Controller to Treasurer and set goals for myself to advance, learn new skills, and develop my strengths as a leader. Knowing I was a minority in this organization both as a woman and an African American drove my determination even more, and I challenged myself to be sure I made my value and presence known.

I was hired as Vice President of Finance for the St. Louis Rams in 1995. From the moment I interviewed for the position to accepting the offer, everything felt right. I immediately felt at home in the St. Louis community, empowered in my position, and felt respected and supported by my colleagues. Or so I thought.

In 2003, I was featured on the cover of *Black Enterprise Magazine*. To be recognized as a leader in the Black community in a publication that celebrates the most accomplished and inspiring Black entrepreneurs and professionals was an honor that still takes my breath away. As news spread of my recognition following the release of the magazine, I was shocked by the response. A Black male colleague confronted me: he held a higher position at the company than me! Why wasn't he the one on the magazine cover?

The pain and disappointment in his sexism stings to this day. To be belittled during one of the most exciting accomplishments of my career was shocking and hurtful. Rather than celebrating a sister, he cut me down.

But there are other times when you don't have to look very far to find an adversary. Sometimes, that person is staring back at you in the mirror.

In 2007, I left the St. Louis Rams for the sunny skies of Phoenix to become the CFO of the Arizona Cardinals. But it turns out there aren't enough palm trees or zeros on your paycheck to make you happy. I soon realized the culture of the Cardinals and Phoenix weren't the right fit for me. I was so unhappy, and the impact was pervasive. My work quality suffered, and my confidence plummeted. I've always been a good motivator for others but I could not seem to dig myself out of this hole. I felt like I was drowning, and I knew I had to make a change or I would lose it all.

In my desperate search for a life preserver, I stumbled upon a webinar by Steven Covey entitled "Writing Your Personal Mission Statement." As I worked through his recommended steps, I identified something in my mission statement that would guide my future: "Inspiring and enhancing the lives of women and girls."

Today, I am back in St. Louis and am living out my greatest title to date: CEO of YWCA of Metro St. Louis. Here, we work tirelessly each day for the empowerment, leadership, and rights of women and girls.

Being a woman has been one of my most defining characteristics from which I derive purpose and strength. It has also been the source of some of the darkest and most frustrating moments in my career, both from others and personally. That's why I'm so passionate about my work today to help support a world where women of any background, any race, in any circumstance can be empowered by being a woman.

I am who I am today because of those three adjectives: Female. First. Black. I am proud of them, I own them, and I am grateful for the journey they've taken me on. In spite of all of the ups and downs, I'm still standing. And I'm standing tall.

ADRIAN E. BRACY began as Chief Executive Officer for YWCA Metro St. Louis in August of 2009. Bracy previously worked as an executive for the St. Louis Rams, then left to become Chief Financial Officer for the Arizona Cardinals. She has more than 18 years of senior management finance experience with professional sports teams, including the Miami Dolphins. Bracy graduated from Morgan State University with a Degree in Accounting and has a Master's Degree in Business Administration from Nova Southeastern University in Ft. Lauderdale, Fla. She has received numerous awards including the St. Louis Business Journal Most Influential Business Woman Award, Black Enterprise 50 Most Powerful Blacks in Sports, and St. Louis American Non-Profit Executive of the Year Award. Bracy is married to Vernon, has a son Donovan, and attends Shalom Church (City of Peace).

Adrian E. Bracy, MBA, CPA

twitter.com/YWCASTL | facebook.com/ywcametrostl

On the Right Track
Ria Ruthsatz

I boarded the roller coaster with such enthusiasm. It was shaped like a giant caterpillar, and the face on the front car smiled in a whimsical way that no three-year-old could resist. The track was a short loop with one very slight drop. The ride was made for children, and I remember being excited that my parents couldn't join me on this one. I buckled in and waved heroically at Mom and Dad. At three years old, I was clearly all grown up.

The excitement built as other children proceeded to board their cars and the carnival music announced the ride was about to begin, but when the caterpillar started down the track I was struck with terror. I panicked and cried for them to let me off, and when they wouldn't, I tried to take matters into my own hands and jump out of my car. In that moment, anywhere was better than wherever that caterpillar was headed.

Thankfully, my parents made them stop the ride before I managed my way out of the buckle, but that was the last time I looked at a rollercoaster with any sort of enthusiasm.

On my 30th birthday I resolved not to let that caterpillar get the better of me, and I braved Space Mountain with my husband. They didn't have to stop the ride, but I still left in tears.

Being an entrepreneur is sort of like riding Space Mountain all day every day. There are unexpected twists and turns, you never truly feel in control, and sometimes you're left in the dark. For someone like me, who likes to know where I'm going and prefers to be in the driver's seat, it can be a constant struggle not to jump.

The unpredictability of running your own business is exactly why I vowed years ago that I would never, ever do it. As a child I watched my parents–both creatives–freelance, and I knew all too well the pains of waiting for the next client to call. When I met my husband, Chadwell, I was once again reminded how hard it is to work for yourself. He was trying to make it as a filmmaker, and watching him handle his own marketing, engage with clients, and deliver a great product was exhausting. Nope, that life wasn't for me. There was a steady predictability to clocking in and working for someone else that I could count on. Sure, there were some ups and downs, but I had a plan, and I could see where I was headed.

So when I suddenly quit my steady job to start a business with my husband, it was as much of a shock to me as it was to everyone else. That decision is perhaps the biggest change I've made to date, and unlike most things in my life, it wasn't the result of careful planning. It was, in fact, due to a change I didn't choose and couldn't have predicted.

Years prior, when we were first dating, Chadwell introduced me to his best friend, Ron. Imagine a young Santa Claus with a red beard and a naughty grin. The twinkle in his eye was a mischievous one, and he had a devil-may-care attitude that was tempered only by his warmth and generosity. He made everyone around him feel comfortable and included, and it wasn't long before I considered him my friend too.

Ron was the first of our friends to buy a house and, like the amazing restaurateur that he was, he hosted much of our lives during those early years. Lazy Sundays were often spent at Ron's, where you could count on great food, fun conversation, and maybe a little trouble. There was really no predicting what Ron might get up to, and that's what made him so much fun.

We would spend entire afternoons talking about his dream to open his own restaurant. He had every detail of the menu planned for every season, and the decor had been meticulously designed right down to the color and thread count of the napkins. I envied his lofty goals. I was beginning to tire of my predictable career track, but I wasn't sure what to do about it.

The years passed, and they were marked by promotions and raises, but I couldn't ignore that nagging feeling that I was stuck on a track leading nowhere. We had our share of happy moments, Chadwell and I got married, but there were fewer and fewer lazy Sundays. We found ourselves replacing childish fun with increasing responsibilities, and those afternoon conversations about future dreams became a rarity. Chadwell was filming more than ever, and Ron had traded his restaurant dreams for a desk job. Ron had hoped the job would be temporary, but with a mortgage and bills to pay it became much longer than he had planned and his restaurant dreams were put on hold.

It's fitting that I received the call on a Sunday. I was working weekends and it was strange that anyone would call me at work. I was sitting at my desk when they told me the news.

Ron had passed away. He was gone. He had died at his desk, at the job he never wanted or planned to have.

The days that followed are a blur, but I know that in that moment everything changed.

We had all spent so much time working toward tomorrow and patting ourselves on the back that we had reached the next step toward something better. We had sacrificed time with our families and with each other, and traded lofty goals for jobs that simply paid the bills. I had spent years trying to plan my life, but I was suddenly faced with the reality that it could end at any moment.

No promotion, raise, or predictable career track was going to give me more time on this earth. I sat at my desk and wondered, what if this is it? What if I don't make it home today? What if the tomorrow I'm working toward never arrives?

There will never be another lazy Sunday at Ron's, and despite my best efforts I still can't recall the last one we had. I like to imagine we all enjoyed it, but the fact is it was just another Sunday —not invested with any significance because we expected to have thousands more.

We couldn't go back and tell ourselves to treasure that last Sunday, but we could change how we treated every moment going forward.

A few short months after Ron passed, I traded my predictable desk for a ride that scared me. I boarded the rollercoaster with more trepidation, but also with conviction. It was no longer enough to go through life simply paying the bills, and we gladly sacrificed all predictability for the chance to pursue bigger dreams.

My husband and I started our own film production company, and six years later I can tell you it has been quite a wild, wonderful, and unpredictable ride. What began as just the two of us working side by side has become a company serving clients around the world.

I am intensely proud of the business and the life we've built, but I'd be lying if I said I didn't shed a few tears along the way. The years have taught me to prepare for the inevitable twists and turns, but the truth is that some days they still get the better of me, and I wish someone would stop the ride and let me off.

Those are the days I think about Ron. I think about all the time we lost while making plans. I think about the futures we imagined on those Sundays, and how different our lives are now from anything we could have predicted. Living in my memory, Ron is the only thing that hasn't changed. He's forever just dreaming and making plans that will never come to be.

I'd give anything for another lazy Sunday and the chance to tell him about the incredible places we've been, the films we've made, and the people we've become. The truth is, it took losing him for any of these things to happen. Thanks to Ron, our years are no longer marked by promotions and raises, and each passing moment is held a little dearer. We're different people now, made braver and more confident with each move down the track.

Nowadays I meet with my clients and discuss their dreams. It's a privilege to hear their lofty ideas and to be a part of sharing their stories with the world. I still don't know what lies ahead, none of us really do, but I do know that we don't have time to waste.

How many plans have you made and then quietly put aside for more practical pursuits?

Those unpredictable twists and turns, ups and downs, that once scared me I now embrace without reluctance. I know that life is short, and each moment may be our last. Without a doubt, I am on the right track. With that in mind, I smile, raise my hands in the air, and enjoy the ride.

RIA RUTHSATZ is Co-Owner and Executive Producer at Tree9 Films, a St. Louis-based commercial film production company whose clients range from local schools and nonprofits to nationally recognized brands. Ria has both produced and directed films around the country, and is proud to have developed fundraising films that have raised millions for important causes worldwide. She and her husband, Chadwell, are true partners both in life and business, and continue to work side by side each day. When she's not filming, Ria is an active member of RISE Collaborative and serves on several local charitable boards and committees that provide opportunities for women at every stage of their professional development.

Ria Ruthsatz

ria@tree9.com

tree9.com | facebook.com/tree9films | linkedin.com/in/riaruthsatz | instagram.com/tree9films

Tick of the Clock
Erin Warner Prange

Many of my childhood memories are a bit fuzzy, or have been somewhat altered by the perspectives of older family members and friends who have since reiterated stories to me about my youth. However, there is one mental image that I hold dear to my heart, and it is sharp as a tack: my mother, dressed up in a fitted blue pencil skirt suit and high heels, with the landline kitchen phone propped up between her ear and her shoulder, taking a pie out of the oven. My sister is in a high chair next to her eating a banana, which places me at four or five years old, but that image has guided me throughout my entire adult life as the epitome of a full-time working mother. I lost my mom about 17 years ago, and as I look back on that picture in our kitchen, it reminds me that time is precious but that she really made the most of hers. And the funny thing is, although she was probably worried that day about making it on time to work, the biggest highlight for me from that scene was how delicious that blackberry pie tasted.

As a constant multi-tasker, the concept of time has always been at the forefront of my mind. There is an ongoing tick of the clock that follows me wherever I go, and of course it usually tells me that I'm running late. My life as a professional dancer has led to a schedule of juggling up to five part-time jobs at a time, and as I've become more and more invested in each of those jobs, the clock seems to tick faster and faster. "The clock" affects everyone in some way: the biological clock, the workday clock, the memo deadline clock, the exercise clock, the sleep clock…There is no way to escape the whirling countdown that surrounds us except to maximize our time and make the best of it…right?

In 2010, I was a professional dancer at The Big Muddy Dance Company when I was asked to take on the additional role of executive director. I knew it would be a huge commitment, but combining my lifelong passion for dance with leading the dance company was a new and exciting challenge that I was ready to take on. However, there was one problem: a huge part of my new role was to raise money and I wasn't a skilled fundraiser. My first assignment came in fast and clear: raise $20,000 in the next two months or we can't afford to pay the dancers.

My stomach turned. Most of the stress was due to the timeline. Two months does not seem like a very long time when you're already pressed for a few minutes here and there, and the insurmountable sum of $20,000 at that point in my career kept bashing me in the head like a ten-pound brick. But I had no choice. I had dancers—friends, colleagues, people passionate about dance just like me—to keep employed and art to produce for this community.

When you're confronted with an impossible task, you have to start small. I decided that instead of cold-calling or asking a wealthy stranger for the full amount, I would begin to learn more about the folks that I thought might be invested in our company's work. I filled my next week with coffee dates and happy hour meetings, and I bought tickets to several local arts events for the next three weeks. I found myself immersed in discussions with arts patrons and business gurus that appeared to me to be the movers and shakers of St. Louis. As I continued to learn more about each person and what made them tick, I found that our dance company had some unique things to offer each individual, and that they might be invested in our cause for a specific reason. One arts patron mentioned that she always wished she was a musician but never fulfilled that dream. She had never attended a dance concert and when I told her that you could almost "see" the music through the dancers' bodies, she became intrigued. A local businessman found interest in our senior citizen outreach program because his mother had Alzheimer's disease and couldn't make it out to see performing arts. One of my old professors came on board with the company as a favor to me and fell in love with the charisma and friendly nature of the dancers. I began talking about the company as if it were my own child and took on the persona of a proud and beaming mama.

As we neared the two-month deadline, we decided to hold a small auction event at our studio space to ask for funds for our choreography and dancers. I was deflated as we set up appetizers and prepared all the gift baskets. Despite my business in the previous months, I had not succeeded in securing the necessary funds. I did not see myself as worthy of my position, nor did I have any idea how to tackle our next month's financial needs. I had learned a great deal about the guests coming to the event that night, but it wouldn't necessarily translate into dollars. My "friend roster" wouldn't help much professionally if our company closed its doors. I'd have to break the news to ten of my best friends that they'd be out of a job in a week.

As people began to stream through the front doors of the studio, I forgot about my predicament. I saw many of the friendly faces from the previous few weeks. Learning details about 100 different personalities and the unique things that made them tick had turned them into good friends for me personally, and I felt as though I were simply at a cocktail party with my favorite people. As we continued throughout the evening, I saw a side of them that made me love them even more. When our auctioneer presented all that our dancers could contribute to the community, hands started to fly up in the air. There was clapping, shouting, laughing, crying… someone walking down the street in downtown St. Louis would never know there was such a blur of excitement happening just upstairs in our tiny studio space. Cue sappy music! Before I could catch my breath, we had raised $21,000 for our new project and had all of a sudden bought our dancers some more time to do what they loved. I was filled with relief and realized relationships will always be the key to success, no matter the timeline.

I continued my balancing act of dancer and executive director for seven more years. My days were crazy but I prided myself on being able to keep all the balls in the air. Then gradually things started to slip. Our organization was growing very quickly and there were infinite emails, deadlines, and meetings that had to be crammed into my half-day after rehearsal. I ended up beginning every conversation with "I'm sorry I didn't get back to you!" I had to accept the fact that I couldn't be the "perfect multi-tasker" and had to make some big changes. I announced to the board that I would retire from dancing and transition to full-time Executive Director at the end of the 2017 season.

And then comes the irony: immediately following my decision to retire, I found out that I was expecting a little one, which pushed my clock as a dancer up significantly. Knowing that I only had a few short months left to do the thing I loved the most, I decided that I would concentrate my efforts on the artistic process and on my relationships with the other dancers rather than the Executive Director tasks I needed to complete after rehearsal each day.

The amazing transformation in me after my attention shifted was astounding. I was able to absorb so much more information and enjoy my time with others in the studio because I was fully present. Instead of watching the clock to anticipate when I'd be able to start my office work, I watched my fellow dancers in appreciation of their beauty. Time seemed to fade away and the focus became the movement and the humanity behind it. By the end of each day, I felt more accomplished, more complete, more inspired to work.

The idea of leaving the clock behind and focusing instead on what makes us tick, and what makes those people around us tick, is easy in theory but extremely difficult in practice. Time has ruled our lives since we learned how to decipher that weird-looking circle with all the numbers. In shifting my view from "when" to "what," I have begun to see that circle in a different way. I now imagine each of my relationships as a pie made up of a thousand slices, each with its own delicious flavor. Every time I have a conversation with someone, give them a smile, share a cup of coffee, those are the slices of pie that contribute to a beautiful, tasty, and full connection.

It is not about when the tick of the clock happens, but what makes us tick as people and how we can build those relationships. How we can fill up our circles with a thousand different flavors to make them the best they can be. How we can discover new things about someone over a cup of coffee…and quite possibly, a piece of blackberry pie.

ERIN WARNER PRANGE Born and raised in St. Louis, Erin Warner Prange holds her B.A. in Dance and Spanish from Colorado State University and her Masters of Fine Arts in Arts Management and Leadership from Webster University. Erin taught dance for the Boston Public School District through the Topf Center for Dance Education, and danced with Fusionworks II in Providence, RI. After returning to St. Louis, she has instructed dance through Trek Dance Collective, Webster Groves High School, the Dance Center of Kirkwood, and the Slaughter Project before joining The Big Muddy Dance Company in 2011. Erin has had the privilege of working with talented artists such as Lou Conte, Brian Enos, Harrison McEldowney, Robyn Mineko Williams, and Robert Moses in her professional dance career. Erin has served as the Executive Director for The Big Muddy Dance Company since 2013.

She currently volunteers as the Advertising Production Manager for Sign of the Arrow charity organization, and serves on the Executive

continued

Committee on the Young Board of Directors for Variety the Children's Charity. She sits on the RISE Society Advisory Board and is honored to work alongside the amazing group of women at RISE.

Erin Warner Prange

thebigmuddydanceco.org

facebook.com/TheBigMuddyDanceCompany

The Serial Achiever
Kerri Mileski

Some call it not knowing what you want to do. Others label it "job hopping" or being a "free spirit." But they've got me all wrong.

For me, my long and diverse list of careers is a sign of "serial achievement."

I have been a dancer, mountain biker, cyclist, runner, insurance claims agent, student, teacher, pastry chef, restaurateur, bakery owner, education director, server, bartender, nutritionist, triathlete, career counselor, trainer, yoga fanatic, compliance evaluator, sales associate, human resource leader, mentor, executive, author, mom, wife, daughter, sister, and believe it or not, more.

I used to be shy—let's be honest, embarrassed—about this list. I dreaded that moment in social settings when an acquaintance would ask about my career. I always seemed to be doing something new or unexpected. Their intention wasn't to be judgmental, but for some reason I took it that way. I think it's because I, too, was wondering if I still hadn't found my calling and was chasing a plan I didn't really have.

At certain points, I definitely was in a one-woman race toward an unknown finish line.

When I was young, I was whimsical, aloof, laid back, and unstructured. It was the 80s, and I was raised by the opposite of today's helicopter parents. There was no talk of career planning; my only expectation was to get good grades and graduate. In my heart I was a hippie mountain biker, so for college I went out to Colorado with a loose plan written on the back of a napkin. And while I ended up with a degree, it might as well have been scribbled on a napkin too.

I recall adults telling me to, "Find my passion," and that would lead to my path. That turned out to be more defeating than inspiring for me. Instead, I just kept going down the road I was on until a new opportunity presented itself. I didn't waste too much time trying to figure out what I really wanted, but instead kept working hard to be successful in my current place, wherever that may be. Each time it was about endurance.

I generated much of my expansive career list from my late twenties to mid-thirties. Several of those roles overlapped— nutritionist, restaurateur, and (first) wife—and were breeding grounds for some of the most painful and profound learning and growing I've done in my life.

As with many fairy tales, this one began with a love story. Swept off my feet, we were aspiring chefs, leading some of the top culinary teams in the best restaurants in the country. We were rich with excitement and ambition, and I learned what it was to be a teammate, leader, and creative force. Unfortunately, I also learned how to completely lose yourself in the spiral of someone else's dreams, instabilities, and ultimately, their addictions.

We moved home to St. Louis and opened our own restaurant venture. It was a whirlwind success for the first year, and life was exhilarating. But I learned that my partner was no partner at all. I learned about deception and betrayal and realized that, even as an owner, you can sometimes find yourself completely out of control.

I remember sitting in my car crying in the parking lot of a grocery store buying bread to serve to our patrons. Our bread vendor refused to deliver to us because we were so far in debt to him. Despite having a full dining room night after night, we didn't have cash to put in the register for change. The numbers weren't adding up, and I realized the only other hand in the register was the one I thought I knew and trusted the most. My husband's.

I went to sleep each night dreading the morning and what uncertainty the next day would bring. I was drowning in stress and anxiety. I knew I couldn't keep going on like this or I would be destroyed—my reputation, my morals, my future. I was already breaking down. I couldn't sit and watch this happen all around me any longer. So I walked away.

Hindsight can always find what we failed to see initially. The signs were there long before we opened the restaurant. I think I knew it wasn't right the day I got married. That this decision wasn't right for me and not where I was supposed to land. Through my winding journey and varied experiences, I've discovered one of my strong traits is endurance and perseverance, even if it's to my own detriment.

As I was picking up the pieces of my life and determining what was next, I was presented with the opportunity to open a bakery. And for all intents and purposes, it should have succeeded. The concept, the demand, the craft were all there. But I had concerns about the partnership and investor arrangement and questioned if the relationship would be a healthy one. I started asking myself whether I really wanted this and soon realized I did not. I was missing the edge, the drive, the passion, and the tolerance. To some extent I had lost my fight. I'm glad I tried, but gosh darnit I wasn't going to go down that road again.

After all of these years of letting momentum guide my way, it was time for me to intentionally find my path. But with such a grab bag of what looked like failed attempts, who would take a chance on me? Did I even know what I was good at?

It's easy to write off the value of an experience when you feel shame about it. Seeing the glass as half full when it was just thrown in your face is tough to do. But after a great deal of self reflection, I was able to put my feelings and insecurities aside and look objectively at my experiences. My time working in the hospitality industry taught me about teamwork and collaboration. I led diverse teams, honed my communication skills, and was innately creative. I could work under intense time pressure, handle high-volume operations, and was a stickler for details.

Even a few part-time sales positions and desk jobs I took along the way taught me to be a quick study, agile, and to build relationships. I had common sense—something I've learned isn't as common as one might think—and that, paired with the ability to learn and adapt, made me an invaluable addition to almost any industry.

I soon became an educator and then a compliance auditor. When I decided to go for my Masters, I found myself not only excelling, but rising as a leader. Others recognized my skills, and fortunately, so did I.

Every experience, every failure, every adventure along the way made me uniquely suited for my current role as a corporate executive overseeing training and human resources. If you would have told 20-something-year-old me that she'd one day be a Chief Human Resource Officer, she would have laughed at you. But that's because she had no idea the growing she'd do.

I am grateful for my experiences, no matter how painful or diverse they may be. They built a foundation that brought me where I am today and is exactly where I'm supposed to be. I learned more in those real-world experiences than I could have learned in any class or from any book. My experiences made me stronger and more confident. I took charge when a relationship or job wasn't healthy for me.

I never had that "lightning bolt" moment. Instead, I tried things. I explored things. Each time, I learned new skills and philosophies, and grew my library of life experiences to draw from. Despite how bad or good some of it felt at the time, it was never wasted time. It got me right where I am supposed to be. Through it all, I found a way to marry the chaos and stability, to manage risk and fear, and let it drive me forward.

I have become proud of my list of achievements. These experiences have become the roots and branches of my tree, growing deeper and expanding wider as I mature. Most importantly, they create a foundation of life moments from which to draw from.

I'm skipping the mid-life crisis. I don't need one. I am going to keep learning, listening, and growing. I look forward to giving back and helping mold others. I now have the husband, family, and career of my dreams. I am still a hippie-mountain-biker-living-in-Colorado kind of girl at heart, and I love my life. But now I have found my calling. I love the people in my world, and I truly love who I have become.

KERRI MILESKI An outdoor enthusiast at heart, Kerri Mileski blends her background in corporate compliance and employee relations with her love for all things active. By day, she's the Chief Human Resources Officer for MTM, Inc., a woman-owned and operated company, leading the company's human resources, training, employee engagement, and performance management teams. After hours, she devotes her time to racing and riding mountain bikes and spending time with her son and husband. Kerri grew up in Missouri and spent time studying Nutrition and Sports Science in Colorado before moving back home. She holds a master's degree in organizational leadership and SHRM SCP certification.

Kerri Mileski

kerrimileski@gmail.com

facebook.com/kerri.mileski | instagram.com/kerrimileski | twitter.com/kerrimileski | linkedin.com/in/kerri-mileski

Gratitude
Ladan Kamfar

On a recent Saturday morning, I was driving with my two sons in the car, windows open and music blaring as we sang along, knowing just half the words but singing loudly nonetheless. There were no cares, no fears—just the sun and the love and the freedom to do, go, and feel whatever we wanted. I couldn't help but smile. Smile because the contrast between my childhood and my kids' is so dramatic, and I couldn't be more grateful.

I was born and raised in Tehran, Iran. When I was young, life was comfortable and happy and our nation was well respected. But after the Iranian Revolution in 1979, our country and our lives fundamentally changed.

What activists thought would be a step forward for our country proved disastrous. We lived under tyranny where nearly every element of our daily lives was policed and dictated by a new and powerful regime. Rights and freedoms were stripped—especially for women. We could be jailed, fined, and even beaten for interacting with the opposite sex, not following strict dress codes, or even listening to music.

I remember when I was 13 years old and my parents had about 40 of their friends over to our house. Mr. G was playing his violin; he was a musical genius who would touch your heart and heal your soul when he played. People were having a great time. We lived on the third floor and suddenly heard the door intercom buzzing.

"Who is this?" my Dad asked.

"Open this door and have everyone come down immediately," responded an angry voice on the other end of the handset. It was the regime guards.

We knew if we went downstairs we could be jailed, and everyone would be whipped and fined for having men and women together. With a split second to make a decision, we all agreed that we were not going down. No way! The Kamfar family was on a mission to save our guests.

My dad went downstairs to talk to the guard. My mom took all the women to the apartment on the second floor. A friend hid all the musical instruments on the rooftop, and I had to make the alcohol and wine disappear. Thinking quickly, I shoved all of the bottles and glasses in my favorite hide and seek spot: the washing machine. Although half of the drinks ended up on my pearl white dress!

Somehow, my dad saved the day, convincing the guards that there were just a bunch of men gathering and watching TV.

It's funny how living under such unforgiving conditions could actually have a positive influence on the kind of person I am today. The regime worked so hard to break my spirit, to tell me that I did not matter, and to make my world so small. But in reality, it made me even more determined to stick to my values, have grit to achieve my dreams, and advocate for equal rights in my life.

I learned from my parents that having an education was not an option, but the only way in life. My father would often say, "A woman must become educated and be able to make a good living." This was a mantra in my head, and I am forever grateful for my father's encouragement and to my mom who modeled that independence for me.

I graduated with a degree in Chemical Engineering from Sharif University of Technology in Tehran. Shortly after my graduation, I knew I had to finally leave the country, and I knew where I wanted to end up: the United States of America.

Since there are no American Embassies in Iran, I traveled to the Embassy on the island of Cyprus to apply for a U.S. visa. When I checked into my hotel, I met the owner named Sandy. She had met many Iranians who come to Cyprus in an attempt to obtain a visa and laughed at my naiveté. That I thought it was possible for a young, single, female Iranian engineer to get a U.S. visa was hilarious to her. They only grant visas to people likely to return home, so as a single woman, I was a long shot.

"Just enjoy the beach, get a tan, and head home, honey," she advised me.

But I was determined. Getting to the United States was the key to my future. The consular, Alan, talked to me for more than 15 minutes, and I think he picked up on my determination, too.

"You know what? I like you," Alan said. "Come back at 3 PM and your visa will be ready. Have fun," he said with a smile. I am forever grateful Alan made an exception for me.

When I first arrived in the United States, introductions were challenging for me and required some emotional detachment. Even the simple question, "Where are you from?" was uncomfortable. It usually went a little something like this:

Them: *"Where are you from?"*

Me: *"I am from Iran."*

Them: *"Where?"*

Me: *"Iran."*

Them: *"Ah! Eye-Ran! Really?! You don't look like an Eye-ranian."*

Me: *"Have you met anyone from Iran?"*

Them: *"No..."*

Me, with a smile: *"Well, they look like me."*

Fast forward to today, I now look forward to meeting new people and sharing my journey with others. Our journey is the essence of the legacy we leave in this world. I truly believe that behind every face, there is an amazing story of challenges and triumphs, and I am excited to share my journey with others and listen to theirs. Being raised in the regime and seeing war for eight years could have crushed my spirit and held back my future, but instead it is the source of my determination to achieve dreams and positivity, and my passion to help others. I am looking forward to a day when the beautiful country of Iran, with all its amazing people, will become free of this tyrannical government. But until that time, I will continue to push forward and possibly change what others think of my country, whether they've met an Iranian or not.

It has now been 20 years since my move to the U.S. My journey has been an amazing path of continuous personal growth, development, and opportunity. I have been with a Fortune 500 company in St. Louis for more than 13 years and held various roles from technical to leading global teams, innovation, and more. I am an entrepreneur coach, a mentor, a public speaker, and the founder of the St. Louis Women in Tech Exchange where women in the technology field share, support, and celebrate one another.

I've learned life offers us many opportunities if we are open to seeing and receiving them. As the international best-selling author, Don Miguel Ruiz, says in his book The Four Agreements, "Don't make assumptions." If we never ask for what we want and if we assume we will not have it, it can never become a reality.

We need to be our own number one advocate. It's that simple: if you want something in life, just go for it. Can you imagine what my life would be like if I assumed I would not get that visa simply because many others are denied?

My journey has led me to be that nudge and reminder for others to show them they are blessed with a life. I choose to see the full half of the glass. I am focused on intentional living and have learned from so many amazing mentors. With the encouragement of a great friend, I started focusing on living a healthier life and have run four half marathons in the past three years.

It is now my passion to mentor, facilitate, and help others become their best selves and live lives of intention. Sometimes we all need a nudge to step into our power. There is no greater feeling of pride and fulfillment than when people step into their power and make magic happen.

If I can share one piece of advice from my experience, it's this: take that next step. Don't overthink or over plan. All we need to do is take that first step and the universe will open so many unexpected doors for us.

As I drive my car now, I can't help but smile. I smile with all of my being about how oblivious my two amazing boys are to how different life can be. And I am filled with the utmost gratitude for the freedom my family has in this country and with love for this land. I will do my best to teach my boys to always live a life of intention. I've learned you aren't always in control of your circumstances but you are always in control of how you respond to them.

"Life is as easy or as hard as you think it is."

LADAN KAMFAR is a visionary technology leader with experience leading highly effective teams focused on Innovation, IT Management, Service Improvement, Business Process Modeling, and Digital Strategy. She is currently the Digital Collaboration Lead at Bayer where she partners with key influencers in the St. Louis region to promote collaborative innovation and digital outreach.

Ladan has passion for facilitation, community empowerment, and building cohesive organizations with a focus on transformational change, team empowerment, continuous improvements and innovative solutions. As a transformation coach, Ladan's vision is to improve lives and empower others to their next level and passionate to connect people and opportunities.

Ladan Kamfar

ladankamfar@gmail.com

facebook.com/ladan.kamfar | twitter.com/ladankamfar | linkedin.com/ladan-kamfar

The Wake Up Call
Heather J. Crider

I t was a long night of tossing and turning, trying to shut my mind down to sleep. Although I've had many sleepless nights, this night was definitely different.

Earlier in the day, one phone call had stopped my future in its tracks and brought everything to a screeching halt.

My best friend, Conrad, and I had been working together tirelessly for several years building a new business. We were both all in and were excited about the future. We trusted one another, and being able to create something that would allow us to remain a part of each other's lives was exciting and important. We had built a growing business, and it was booming!

The business led me to security and financial freedom, and it was exhilarating to see my hopes and dreams finally coming true.

But that changed. With one phone call, it was over.

The phone call from Conrad, who was disgusted and displeased that I couldn't be reached the prior day, went something like this:

"Heather, when I call, I expect you to answer. I've been trying to get ahold of you for a whole day now."

But this day, it hit me that I was chained to being "on call" with him, and I'd had enough of it. No more. I wasn't going to answer to him every second of the day.

I had been pushed too far.

The real tipping point for me was a few weeks prior when I'd told Conrad that my son had a baseball game and I wouldn't be able to make a webinar. He'd screamed at me, saying he didn't care if my son had a game and that Little League baseball was not going to interfere with his business making money (Note that he used the word "his" for our business).

Hold on a second! Since when am I an employee? And what did he mean Little League doesn't matter? It matters to me and my family, so it should matter to my business partner and best friend.

After that, I knew things needed to change dramatically. I thought about walking away, but the consequences were paralyzing. My kids and I were becoming accustomed to a comfortable new life. Why did I feel so afraid? The business was partly mine, after all.

I realized I had been bullied for a long time. Lies were being told, and I believed them. Lies like, "Outside of me, you don't have much else going on and you can't make it without me," Conrad would say.

Who says this, and more importantly, who listens? I listened. That's why I was so angry and scared to walk away. I was afraid of failure and afraid of being wrong. Afraid to change, again.

Back to the infamous phone call.

The moment he aggressively muttered those arrogant words to me, without flinching or giving it a second thought, I was triggered. "I will no longer tolerate being treated this way," I shot back. "You don't control me and won't speak to me like this. I don't answer to you."

Then, I did the unthinkable. I hung up.

A text came through: "No one hangs up on me. If you don't call me in the next three minutes to apologize, I will never speak to you again and you are no longer welcome in my life."

My first thought was, "Good riddance. I'm free!" But then reality hit. "Oh #&*!, now what?!"

I had no idea how to move forward, nor any way to collect on accounts receivable. He had managed to control all the accounts and move everything slowly into his name. The original business was zeroed out and I would no longer have access to income.

So what happened? I walked away from it all to save my soul and, as a result, I suffered financially and emotionally. My security and freedom were gone. Few people knew the real hell I was going through, nor did I want them to. I was hurt, scared, and betrayed. Truthfully, I felt like a victim and I blamed him. Yet I was too ashamed to admit the entire truth.

After a lot of dark days and self-loathing, I had to take a hard look at myself. I knew he was toxic, but I allowed myself to feel trapped and powerless. I was like the metaphorical frog who immediately jumps out of a pot of boiling water, but will sit in a pot of water slowly raising in temperature until it dies. I realized that I only speak up when I am pushed too far.

Now came the real self discovery. Luckily for me, one of my passions is understanding the brain and how our thoughts shape our success.

What I reflected upon and learned about myself was that, in some ways, I craved the energy this volatile and toxic relationship produced.

Our brains become addicted to familiarity. It becomes our new normal for survival. This volatility I had quickly become accustomed to was sadly familiar from other times in my life. This pattern was my pattern and it had to change.

But how? How do we possibly change a pattern that is so ingrained into our personalities?

Change starts with acknowledgment in what we believe.

Just acknowledging it happened and how I felt was important. I had to be completely honest with myself about the business, the situation, my gut instincts, and my involvement.

It was really hard for me to accept this. I felt that accepting it meant it wasn't significant, but that simply isn't true. Accepting and honoring myself, as well as owning up to my thoughts and feelings, made it possible for me to understand what I should change.

Yet I still doubted myself. I felt like a fraud, pretending to be the person other people saw me as. Even after everything that happened, people still viewed me as successful. But who the heck am I to talk about success? I'm not perfect enough to be called a success.

I've had quite a few failures in my life and thought those failures meant I wasn't qualified to offer help to anyone. This was my internal conversation.

Once I understood where all of these messages came from and why I believed what I did, I could see my patterns and better understand my beliefs.

It was then that I was able to create a new vision for myself, with new thoughts and beliefs. The goal was to envision the person I knew I was meant to be so I could start thinking and acting like that person. And then I was able to actually become that person.

This process of self discovery is ongoing. I am now not only successful, but so much more whole and fulfilled, and I have a new appreciation for myself, others, time, freedom, and money.

In fact, this entire journey has helped me add to what I've always loved doing and grow a new business. These hard-learned lessons are now a foundational piece to several programs I created that help others push through challenges and become more successful.

The realization that day from "the big phone call" was that I chose this. I chose to walk away and put myself first. To stand up and not take the licks. To push forward despite the fear. I chose to live fully and be present. That day, I said "Yes" to me, and I'm so proud I did!

Because of this journey, I finally had the courage to create a program I've dreamt of for many years, titled "Go Reflect Yourself"!

Through the program, business owners master their own internal messaging, as well as the messages they create to attract clients and prospects. I help them understand their self-imposed limitations and how success can be sabotaged by our experiences and thinking. The program allows for structured reflection as participants learn to push past barriers and become more successful than ever. Together, we create connected messages with which business owners can flourish, ultimately leading to extraordinary fulfillment and business success.

As a result, not only do people sleep all night long, but they also find themselves jumping out of bed every morning ready to take on the day with joy, vigor, and a newfound enthusiasm similar to what children have on Christmas morning. And I do too, because I've lived it and practice what I preach! No more tossing and turning; I sleep like a baby.

HEATHER J. CRIDER is the founder of Heather J. Crider & Company and Digital Architect Media. She is a keynote speaker, Google Certified Partner, as well as a Master Business Strategist and author of The Digital Marketing Success Formula.

Heather specializes in helping business owners break through their own inner doubts to master the art of the sales conversation. One of her main passions and hobbies is a dedication to and study of neuroscience and how the relationship with our own brain helps us achieve success in business and our personal lives. Because of this passion, she has been trained and certified in numerous personal development, leadership, mindfulness, marketing, and transformational programs. This has led her to create sales and marketing programs, as well as a personal success program titled *Go Reflect Yourself.*

continued

Heather is a proud single mom of two and no stranger to overcoming the trials and tribulations it takes to run a successful business. While founding and growing four successful companies in the financial and marketing industries, she has amassed a wealth of experience and knows what it takes to make things work.

Heather J. Crider

heatherjcrider.com | digitalarchitectmedia.com | goreflectyourself.com

The Chicken Incident

Joy Roberts

I will never forget the day: sitting in rush hour traffic, driving from one job to the other, tears pouring down my cheeks because I couldn't decide what to make for dinner with my girlfriends. I was anxious and freaking out...over dinner.

My friends and I use our commutes to and from work to catch up about the week's events. On this particular day, it was my friend Jen and I who found time to connect. Topics usually included the light ones you might expect from thirty-somethings: How has your week been? How are the kids? When will I see you next? I need wine. I miss you! Let's grab coffee soon and also...wine!

But on this particular day, Jen was greeted with my sobs. When she discovered the source of my emotional turmoil, she did what any good friend would do. She said, in as supportive a way as she could (while trying not to laugh, I'm sure), "Dude, throw some chicken in the Crock-Pot and call it a day."

We all have those times, right? I mean, life is hard. It gets to us. It wears us down and before we know it, we're alone in our car crying about chicken. But "The Chicken Incident" was part of a much larger picture for me. A picture that included a lifelong struggle with anxiety, a failed career, shame and embarrassment over that failed career, and the certainty that I would never be able to fix it. Although I didn't know it at the time, that Crock-Pot full of chicken was the start of a new chapter.

Anxiety has been a part of my life for as long as I can remember. Worry and panic were all too common feelings for me. I have had "chicken incidents" my entire life. If the situation was new, different, changing, or out of my control, I was worried about it. I had a constant, nagging feeling that things were going to go wrong, always with catastrophic consequences. Perspective was a stranger. I would get sick. I would cry. I would have a panic attack and sometimes I couldn't breathe. Over time, I learned to avoid anything that I even suspected would bring on these feelings. Staying in the status quo was the only way I knew how to protect myself.

On the outside, I was "normal" (whatever that means). Looking at me, you would never guess the struggle and inner turmoil that lingered. I was popular, stayed active, and got good grades. I was a Sweetheart Princess and co-captain of the cheerleading squad for crying out loud! But I was really good at masking my symptoms. I managed to be what everyone expected of a teenage girl.

Unfortunately, I could only pull off that charade for so long. College was a difficult transition for me and as the pressures of college increased, my symptoms worsened. During a time in which most students are partying and enjoying the freedoms from home, I relied on the security blanket of my family to help ensure I could get through those four years.

With my newly framed Psychology degree (oh, the irony), I was off to graduate school. I was getting pretty good at sustaining my "normal" façade, so instead of letting anyone know I was struggling, I decided to make a career out of helping those who were. I was going to be a therapist!

Graduate school was probably the most eye-opening experience for me. It was not college. Graduate school was serious business. Everyone else had it all figured out. Meanwhile, I was full of more self-doubt and fear than ever.

This is the real deal. What if I fail? What if I'm going to be a terrible therapist? I don't belong here. What will everyone think if I quit?

I ignored those negative voices and I stayed. I finished my Master's in Social Work. It was rough but I survived and was on my way.

I guess this is the part where I thought it would all come together. I finished college and graduate school despite my fears and anxiety. Surely I would be able to continue this act into my first job and no one would know the help I actually needed myself.

But it was 2009 and the economy sucked! It seemed no amount of networking or interviews would help me find a job, so it became 18 months of rejection letters, emails, and unreturned phone calls.

My anxiety was at an all-time high. There's nothing quite like repeated rejection that nurtures self-destructive feelings of fear, failure, and self-doubt. For me, those feelings took over, and when

I was finally offered a position, my confidence and self-assurance were so low that I eventually resigned from that job, convinced I didn't have what it took.

I wasn't meant to help people. I was right all along. I didn't belong and now I had the evidence to prove it.

The next several years weren't all that bad. I had a fallback option: my family owned a company that I went to work for. I'm sure you're thinking to yourself, "Well, that's lucky." You are welcome to call it luck. I call it a blessing and a curse. A blessing because my family worked hard to build something sustainable and I got to be a part of it. A curse because I no longer had any reason to even think about pursuing my dream of and passion for being a therapist.

I got comfortable learning the ropes at my family's business. Accounting was my new forte and I was actually really good at it. Helping people and social work were a distant memory. I was content. My symptoms were at bay. I wasn't worried or scared anymore. I was safe.

I was also angry. What was it about feeling comfortable and content that made me so angry?

That's the tricky thing about shame. It's a master of disguise. I was mad at everything and everyone. Mad at my family for welcoming me into the business, and furious at anyone who dared to ask why I was working in the family business and not doing social work.

What did they care? Who are they to judge? I don't owe anyone an explanation, I thought. Except I didn't have a good explanation, and saying the words, "I gave up," was too painful.

Remember Jen from "The Chicken Incident?" One day she asked me, "Are you talking to anyone?"

"You mean, like, a therapist?!? Shh! Don't say that out loud!" I protested.

Therapy is bad. It means I'm weak. Buck up. Deal with it. Therapy was meant for all the people I was going to help way back when. It was not meant for me.

Except that it *was* meant for me. Therapy saved me. Saved me from the shame and embarrassment of my failed career attempt. Saved me from the anger and resentment of blaming my circumstances on everyone in my life. Therapy saved me from myself.

I truly believe God brought my first therapist, Justine, into my life. I never expected to sit in her office, give the Cliff's Notes version of my life, and hear her say, "I feel that way, too."

What?! She's the therapist with a successful private therapy practice. She actually made something of herself. How could she possibly know about shame and embarrassment and anger and resentment?

That was the first time I realized everyone has a story to tell. Her story was different but the feelings were the same. You know what else I learned that day?

Stories can be rewritten.

Learning to control the narrative of my story was not easy. It was painful. It hurt, and it was the most uncomfortable I've ever been. I had to dig deep. Up until this point, nothing about my story felt authentic. I was masking everything and playing it safe. It was time to create meaning from my experiences—not from a place of shame and failure, but from a place of love, worthiness, and value.

I took every last experience I could think of and learned to be thankful for it. I learned gratitude. I learned that anxiety was really my superpower! My anxiety allowed me to feel and empathize in a way that was rare and that I didn't realize was possible. I had changed the narrative. I was no longer ashamed of my experiences. For the first time, I felt satisfied. Proud, even.

When Justine's career took her in a different direction, I found my current therapist, Mika, who continues to be an essential and influential person in my life. Mika teaches me to harness the superpowers that my anxiety actually provides. She continues to remind me to be nice to myself, and helped me realize that a career in helping people is still possible and within reach. With her help, I am a social worker again, and I am pursuing my dream of opening a private therapy practice one day.

My story isn't over. Actually, now that I'm doing what I love, doing what I was put on this Earth to do, my story is just beginning.

JOY ROBERTS is a Social Work Case Manager for SSM Health Behavioral Health at DePaul Hospital in St. Louis, an inpatient mental health service that exists to help heal mind, body, and spirit of all ages. Prior to beginning her work in social work, Joy worked in corporate and construction accounting for her family's small specialty construction company, Roberts Loading Dock. A graduate of St. Louis University's School of Social Work, Joy is skilled in clinical assessments and investigations, and did so for the Federal Public Defender of the Eastern District of Missouri for the purpose of utilizing assessments in order to advocate for fair sentencing during criminal defense cases.

Joy's own struggle with anxiety lead her to the field of social work. She is passionate about upholding her Christian values in her social work practice, about helping those who often feel helpless, and making sure everyone knows there is always somewhere to turn.

When she isn't following the St. Louis Cardinals or Kansas Jayhawks basketball team, Joy can be found spending time with her family, friends and friends' kids. These are the relationships she holds dearest and she wouldn't be where she is today without them.

Joy Roberts

jeroberts31@hotmail.com

facebook.com/jeroberts31 | linkedin.com/in/joyelizabeth31

ε

Passing the Torch
Mentoring and Professional Success
Amy Hoch Hogenson

I recently attended an event where Associate Justice Sonia Sotomayor of the United States Supreme Court spoke about her new children's books, which detail many of her exemplary accomplishments. At this talk, she said she does not believe people who say they are self-made because no person is self-made. Each of us is made with the help and support of others.

She could not be more right.

My own hard work allowed me to graduate from college a year early. I put myself through law school, passed the bar exam, and now practice alongside some of the best lawyers in St. Louis. But I will readily admit I did not do it alone. At every stage of my journey, I have been mentored, guided, and taught by people that have shaped me, inspired me, supported me, and helped me to overcome adversity. Looking back at my journey, I am compelled to recognize the women and men who supported me along the way and to share the impact a mentor can have.

As a college student, I was intrigued by an introductory philosophy class led by Dr. Thomas Simon, an intelligent, patient, happy, and passionate teacher. After taking his Philosophy 101 class, that intrigue became a fascination, and I decided to minor in philosophy and continue to take Dr. Simon's more complex courses.

He eventually invited me to be his teaching assistant during my senior year, and I found remarkable impact in working alongside him.

I discovered Thomas was a non-practicing lawyer. We spent a lot of time talking about the journey from LSAT to law student to lawyer, and he helped me unpack what I really wanted from my chosen career: the impact I wanted to make, what I was passionate about, where my authentic strengths would serve me best. As I was finishing college and applying to law schools, he helped me narrow my options based on what was best for me, my goals, and my personality.

Soon I met a fork in the road with an opportunity to instead pursue an MD/JD program that would make me both a doctor and a lawyer. I knew just who to turn to for advice. Thomas helped me recognize that my passion to be a lawyer far exceeded my desire to practice medicine. After lengthy conversations with him about what was really right for me, I chose the law, and I regret nothing about that choice. I learned true determination, focus, and authenticity.

How fortunate that after 20 years and countless requests for advice, Thomas and I are still friends. We keep in touch and see each other as often as possible.

With Thomas' apt guidance, I attended law school at St. Louis University. It was everything I had hoped for and more. In the summer of 2000, I competed for a coveted position as a summer associate. I landed at Helfrey, Simon & Jones. That summer position turned into an impactful seven years with some of the most generous attorneys and partners I've known (Phil Graham, Paul Simon, Mark Gonnerman, David Helfrey, John McCullough, David Jones, Douglas Roller, and David Neiers) in a place where I would learn two important lessons that fundamentally shaped me.

I learned to be assertive in a civil and polite way—something not all attorneys are known for. I remember Phil preparing me for our first meeting, something called a "status conference," with a judge. He stressed the importance of speaking first, but doing so politely. His words—"Get your story out first!"—echo in my mind and make me smile each time I follow this advice.

Law school does not prepare you for the realities of a lawyer's life. I was a young naïve lawyer and in many ways, these attorneys served as parents to me. They were patient, taking time to help me understand each new project. They had open-door policies and always appeared happy to help despite their own demanding schedules. That patience was a gift and a lesson to me then and is something I now work to give to myself and others each day.

After seven years of working for Helfrey, Simon & Jones, a new opportunity arose at Paule, Camazine & Blumenthal, where I am currently a principal. I will, however, always be grateful for those critical lessons from my first professional mentors.

Although new to Paule, Camazine & Blumenthal, I already had an interesting history with one of my bosses, Alisse Camazine. Alisse and I crossed paths early in my career when we were opposing counsel and had a phone call to discuss the case. She was a seasoned veteran so I came to our call ready to prove I was no pushover. As we spoke, Alisse began to raise her voice louder and louder. After some time, I'd had enough. She couldn't talk to me like that! I told her I was not going to talk to her if she was going to yell at me...and I hung up on her!

I laugh about this now because anyone who knows Alisse knows she just speaks very loudly; it's part of her personality and reflects her incredible passion and intensity. Alisse and I eventually "made up," and in the years since, she has become far more than a colleague—she is also a mentor and dear friend. Alisse is strong, passionate, prepared, diligent, and never stops.

When I was pregnant with my daughter, I worked as hard as I did pre-pregnancy. I ran to court too often, got overheated, and fainted in a courtroom one day. Without telling me, Alisse gathered the lawyers in our office and had an "intervention" she felt was necessary to slow me down. My initial displeasure with her trying to limit what I could do turned into gratitude, as I realized the depth of her concern and that of my colleagues. Alisse taught me that being a true leader means taking care of your team and yourself.

My law partners and I have also gone through many personal difficulties, including the loss of a spouse, serious illness, and the loss of parents. Through it all, Alisse tirelessly steps in to shore up what is important in each of our lives. I have learned so much from her about the importance of priorities. What and who we are outside of our firm is just as important—if not more—as our work.

Also present on my first day at Paule, Camazine & Blumenthal was an inspirational woman named Susan Block. I knew Susan well by the time I joined the firm—I had been pleading cases to her as a judge for most of my career. Susan was the first elected female magistrate in St. Louis County and someone I admired greatly as a woman in the legal profession. But after 25 years on the bench, Susan took the untraditional path of going into practice. While it's unusual to plead to someone then practice alongside them, I consider myself lucky to have done so.

Now working side by side, I have grown both professionally and personally with Susan's encouragement. More seasoned in my career, I was ready to get more involved within the legal community, so I reached out to Susan for guidance on supporting my growth. She connected me with a number of industry organizations and introduced me to some of the greatest minds in our industry. Soon, I made one of my most daring moves yet: I ran for a St. Louis County Judicial Commission position, which stretched and challenged me, and I wouldn't have attempted without Susan's encouragement.

I've also grown personally since meeting Susan, thanks to her emphatic belief in philanthropy, community support, and involvement. She helped me find boards where I could be actively involved and has reminded me about the importance of "giving back" through her own public service for countless organizations. And she constantly demonstrates the importance of our own individual reputation. What you do, what you say, and how you act makes an impact on how people respect you. She could not be more right.

The list of others who have impacted my life is never-ending. But now it's my turn to make an impact. I have realized that while I can still learn from my law partners, I can also help guide and teach the next generation. A former high school intern, Sammie Jones, recently joined our firm as an associate and became my mentee. I feel incredibly fortunate to pass along some of my mentors' lessons to her. My role from student to teacher has come full circle.

I believe we get what we give. I have no doubt that I am a strong, confident, ethical, prepared, empathetic, and methodical family law attorney because I had the support of my mentors throughout the journey. I relish becoming a mentor and I look forward to the years of teaching ahead.

AMY HOCH HOGENSON is an attorney and partner at Paule, Camazine & Blumenthal. Amy works exclusively in the area of family law. Her areas of specialty are divorce (including high-conflict custody cases), post-divorce enforcement, adoption, paternity, grandparents' rights, and prenuptial agreements. In addition to her private practice, Amy also volunteers as a Special Private Prosecutor for the domestic violence court in St. Louis County; as attorney for Legal Services of Eastern Missouri; as a volunteer attorney for The Kaufman Fund; and volunteer attorney for Safe Connections.

Amy is a graduate of St. Louis University School of Law, where she served as managing editor of the *St. Louis University Public Law Review* and captain of the Jessup Moot Court team. Amy currently serves on the Board of The Sheldon and Food Outreach. She is involved as a Fundraising Committee Member of Caring for Kids, and a previous board member for Urban Future. Amy is the recipient of

continued

the 2012 Women's Justice Award for Rising Star and Super Lawyers "Rising Star" for 2009, 2014, 2015, 2016 and 2017; Super Lawyers 2018, and named to Best Lawyers in America for 2019.

Amy resides in University City, Missouri with her husband and two children.

Amy Hoch Hogenson

ahogenson@pcblawfirm.com

www.pcblawfirm.com

Out of the Ashes
Holly Cunningham

September 11, 2001

Autumn sunlight streamed into the living room of my charming little home in the suburbs of St. Louis. Through the windows I could see the leaves on the maple trees beginning to turn colors. Life was good: I was pregnant with twin girls, my catering business was on its feet. Nothing stood in my way.

One of my employees, who had an office in my home, knocked on my bedroom door. "Holly, have you seen the news?"

I had not. I followed her and sat on the edge of a footstool in the living room. Together, we watched the horrifying events unfold.

Twenty minutes later, the Twin Towers were reduced to ashes. My heart ached and I felt paralyzed. I'm not sure exactly when I got up and dressed that day—it's such a blur and yet I'll never forget it—but somehow, we moved forward.

Our country, our world, our humanity were forever changed. What I didn't anticipate was that 9/11 would impact my budding business, too. Early on, my company was built on corporate holiday gifts. In the aftermath of 9/11, we all began giving to charities and trying to help our communities however we could. An unintended result of this, however, was that my business sales dipped dangerously low that season. I had also just leased our first location and was spending thousands on a new kitchen buildout. Things were tight and tense to say the least.

We survived that holiday season and in February, my twins were born. I stayed home a month and then went right back to work. It took some coordination and more than a little teamwork to keep the family and business running smoothly (or at least look like we were). Were it not for the babysitter I found in the Photo Department of Walgreen's, I'm not sure how we would have managed!

Even though the business was struggling, I focused on marketing and it paid off. That spring, although things still looked bleak, Hollyberry Baking and Catering Company won three local business awards in a row, catapulting it to the next level. It kept growing and growing...

Fast forward 12 years. My twins were in middle school, and my company was thriving. I had everything I had hoped and worked so hard for. But there was one problem.

I was bored.

I thought about other career options. I even had a dream about a window. I remember it was small and high up in a room. I knew that window had significance, I just didn't know what it was—yet.

At first I thought it meant I had a window of time to do something else. Sort of an early midlife moment, I suppose. For an exhilarating few days, I imagined being free of owning a business, going to coffee with my friends, wearing a sweatshirt and leggings, and just "finding myself." (I don't think I'm alone in these business owner fantasies, right?)

But I could not fantasize for long. My lease was up and my landlord had given me a deadline to sign a one-year contract at our current location. We were on a month-to-month lease and it was time to commit or move on. I reluctantly signed the document since I had no new direction at this point, and set it on my landlord's desk.

About an hour later, I saw a "For Lease" sign on a really interesting retail building in a great location. I pulled into the lot and called. It was a good price, and my heart began to pound. Was this too good to be true or destiny?

I called my Office Assistant to have her go next door to the landlord's office to retrieve the signed contract. But it was too late... he was there with my signed lease in hand.

I begged and he eventually relented. We were back on a month-to-month lease until I could decide if this new location was the right one. I also needed to determine if that window in my dream was a window of opportunity within my business or without it.

As I mulled over my future, I had the opportunity to get away for a girls' weekend in Seattle with some college friends. We rented an old, quirky house (lots of hippie vibes) with a fabulous back deck. We gathered our food and beverages and started to catch up.

I had been mulling over a new concept to expand my business into something new—to open a "window" within the business—and decided this would be a perfect opportunity to get some feedback. I knew my friends would tell me the truth, as they were my perfect target audience.

These women—a dance teacher, a research scientist, and a marketing director—had known me for more than 20 years. All were busy moms who prided themselves on fixing good food and entertaining with class. And all of them craved more quality time for themselves and their families.

I shared my idea—to take my existing business and build a new brand out of its roots. A brand that had a mission to help busy people eat good food—locally prepared and family friendly—thereby gaining more time and finding more meaning in their busy lives.

Drumroll, please...

They loved it, and Nourish by Hollyberry was born.

Then I really had to get to work. My team and I decided that the new location we found was the right one, but I faced real self doubt. Were my college friends and I the only ones who would be interested in this? I needed a bigger test with potential customers.

So I called in the troops: 100 local, powerful, busy women from all walks of life whom I trusted to help me understand the St. Louis buying market as it related to prepared foods and party food. I hosted hard-hat parties in our unfinished space, gave presentations, handed out surveys, and started a crowdfunding campaign that raised more than $25,000.

It was exhilarating and also tremendously overwhelming. I had to negotiate the new lease, build out a new facility with a retail market vibe, and launch a new brand, not to mention try to keep the rest of my business running while maintaining a healthy lifestyle for my family.

In April of 2015, we opened our new facility with lots of prayer and hope for a new beginning. The new space combined our catering kitchen, our offices, and the Nourish by Hollyberry Market.

From the time I watched the Twin Towers crumble on that TV in my living room to now, I discovered that no matter what was going on in the world or in my own life, in order for my business to survive I had to be nimble and creative in spite of significant challenges, many of which would be beyond my control.

I also realized that I wanted to be part of a bigger vision that brings families together and gives them more time to enjoy each other. Life is uncertain and time is our greatest gift. While Hollyberry Catering helps families celebrate life events, Nourish helps families carve out more time for each other on a daily basis.

Now, a couple of years into Nourish by Hollyberry and almost 20 years since the inception of Hollyberry Baking and Catering, there are days I cannot believe the obstacles we have overcome. We have survived failed employee hires, our space almost flooding, power outages, and a fire during the busy holiday season...and those are just the recent ones! We have also expanded into the space next door (with a prayer we will keep growing!), revamped the brand three times, overhauled the software and website, and worked with three (yes, three) different marketing firms to help make our dreams come true!

Nourish by Hollyberry has gone from being a simple idea for a retail market selling family-friendly meals to capitalizing on the meal-subscription trend and serving more people by delivering healthy, delicious, convenient meals right to their door, and Hollyberry Catering has grown to be one of the top caterers in St. Louis.

Throughout all of the changes and challenges, I'm thankful for what we have learned. We have created a positive team of employees who enjoy working together toward the goal of creating good food and good fun.

There have been times when I have wondered if I made the right decision to continue, but I know that nothing worth having is easy. And I also know that no matter what is going on in the world, where you are in your career, your family, or even your mood, you can reinvent yourself and your business if you have enough faith and passion—and the help of a few good friends.

HOLLY CUNNINGHAM founded Hollyberry Baking Company in 1998 to leverage her lifelong love of cooking to provide made-from-scratch baked goods for corporate gifts. In 2001, the company expanded to add Hollyberry Catering to provide creative menus for corporate and social events. Under her leadership and according to The St. Louis Business Journal, the company has grown to become one of the largest catering companies in the St. Louis area. In 2016, Cunningham opened Nourish by Hollyberry, St. Louis' first family-friendly meal subscription service and prepared foods market.

Holly passionately believes that good food begets togetherness—for families, communities, and corporations. Her creations have been recognized by Sauce Magazine, The Knot, Paula Deen, and Rachael Ray. A St. Louis native, she also is also passionate about supporting the community. Her companies' "Gifts that Give Back" program

continued

has benefitted organizations including SSM Cardinal Glennon Children's Medical Center and Big Brothers Big Sisters of Eastern Missouri. Most recently, Holly partnered with Pink Ribbon Girls to help provide meals to women who have been diagnosed with breast and gynecological cancers in St. Louis and surrounding areas.

Holly strives to be warm and inspiring to those around her; she credits her Hollyberry team, her family, friends, and her faith for her success.

Holly Cunningham

facebook.com/HollyberryCatering | facebook.com/NourishbyHBerry | instagram.com/hollyberycatering

instagram.com/nourishbyhollyberry | linkedin.com/company/hollyberry | linkedin.com/in/holly-cunningham

It's a Millennial!

Lynne Hayes

L ittle did I know that on December 1, 1988, I was giving birth to a millennial.

The first question I asked when Emmy was born was, "What kind of baby is it?" This was pre-everyone finding out the gender of their baby and revealing it in an astonishing way, which I think has taken the fun out of delivery day. I honestly didn't know if I was having a boy or a girl. What if, instead of saying, "It's a girl!" the doctor had looked over his glasses at me and announced, "It's a millennial!"

How would that have changed the way I raised my kids? If only I had known then what an impact millennials would have on our society. Officially the largest generation, the way millennials think, act, spend, and communicate has shaken things up. It's funny to think how almost 30 years ago, we weren't thinking about millennials—not about how we raised them differently than other generations, not about living with them, not about working with them—and yet here we are trying to figure out how multiple generations can live and work together.

And to think all I wanted was a baby!

While Emmy was growing up and becoming a full-fledged millennial, I was hard at work in the corporate world dealing with being a busy working mom, juggling a full-time career, and all of the responsibilities that came along with that. I spent many years dealing with everyday work issues, coaching and mentoring others, and building up those "wisdom" skills that I like to think helped me raise my children into the humans they are today; these skills make them a little different than your stereotypical millennial.

From a very young age, Emmy and her brother Sam (also a millennial) were well-loved, well-coached children of what I liked to say was a "happily married single-parent family." My husband and I both traveled extensively for our jobs throughout our children's formative years, yet we were always able to make sure one of us was around. In a time before today's constant stream of communication, we weren't FaceTiming and Instagramming and texting. No, we were calling each other and leaving messages on landline answering machines and, if we had them, our brick-shaped cell phones.

Somehow, we managed to raise them to adulthood without many calamities. Emmy and Sam knew that if they had a problem at school, I would be the first one to help them, but only if they came to me with the truth, what they had tried or thought of trying, and what their role in the situation was. I was never one of those moms running to the rescue.

Asking them for the truth and holding them accountable helped them in so many ways, especially when it came to them not having an undeserved sense of entitlement like many millennials (Sam's words, not mine). From an early age, they were taught to see both sides of every situation and work toward a mutual solution.

Now don't get me wrong, we still had our share of dilemmas and emotional meltdowns, especially in junior high when the hormones were raging and the kids were all trying to figure out their place in the world.

While it seems we should have left all of that nonsense behind in our youth, I can't help but think that work feels a little bit like junior high sometimes, don't you think?

Hormones and popularity contests aside, I came to discover that as Emmy navigated her way through school and into the workforce and she (luckily) turned to me in good times and bad, the decades between us and the "wild differences" the media would have you believe there was between a boomer and a millennial weren't quite that different after all.

Take our first jobs, for example. Even though our start dates were more than 30 years apart, our experiences and feelings were eerily similar. Hard to believe, but I was young once with all of the same anxieties and fears of other generations before me!

Will I be able to do the work? Will I like my boss? Will I ever have another day of fun in my life?!

All legitimate questions that have been asked by new professionals for many generations. We both dealt with that mournful feeling that college was over, our youth was gone, and we could never go back. In fact, I still feel that way at the beginning of every school year!

I had a tough female boss and so did Emmy. They were both relentlessly fierce and terrifying at the same time. We both learned a lot from these women: they were tough and fair. They taught us to be accountable, do what needed to be done, and make hard decisions without looking back. Some of my earliest bosses formed my understanding of being an influence on others, and that people are watching you. This is a lesson that we all need to learn.

As a new employee in the workforce, my bosses were of a different generation, but I don't remember being labeled a "baby boomer" at that time. We were just new hires. The members of older generations left it to us to become the "labelers"—to label an entire generation as millennials, put them all in one bucket together, and try decide what to do with them!

I've raised millennials, worked with millennials, and led a team of millennials, and here's what I've learned: in general, they are a wonderful generation, full of hope and promise. I've also learned that they have been left with some challenges from previous generations that they will need to figure out. There are plenty of unfair mindsets and stereotypes surrounding millennials and plenty of work we all need to do to get along and thrive in the workplace.

One of the stereotypes I've heard a lot is that millennials are lazy. No. They're not. This is like saying all people with brown eyes are lazy. (I have brown eyes BTW.) Millennials are as hardworking and ambitious as any other generation. They just need to be challenged in the workplace and know that their work matters. As Emmy was finding her place in the workforce, she put in plenty of hours, sacrificing many nights of sleep to make deadlines. She worked hard to make her job the best it could be.

The team of millennials I led were the same. They wanted to know what was next. They asked for more responsibility. They asked for more money. Were they a little overly confident and ambitious? Maybe. But I would rather have to work on channeling an ambitious team than try to get a team to do their work.

We all need to remember that we were young once. Generations start looking more alike the longer they are in the workforce.

Emmy and I have embarked on a partnership that we're calling "Let's Work on Work," or WOW for short. The idea of working together on work came from a relationship between us that's been more than a typical mother-daughter relationship; it's been more like a coach-mentor relationship (with a lot of love) from both sides. We feel like we have an opportunity and a unique perspective to share some of the things we've learned. We've spent hours talking together at home and on our podcast about generational issues in the workplace. We've created content and a meaningful workshop to help others because we realize it's more about how we're the same than how we're different. To work on generational issues in the workplace, we have to stop stereotyping. Look at each individual for who they are and what they bring to the team, and see how they fit into the bigger picture. Learn how they like to work, how they like to communicate, and what their hopes and dreams are.

Acknowledge millennials often and from your heart. This is one place where baby boomers (yes, that's me too) need to take responsibility. We raised these kids with lots of adoration and praise, to think they were the best (and of course they are!), so that's what they expect in life and in the workplace. That ship has sailed so we now need to spend more time communicating and offering feedback to our millennial generation in the workplace.

I say, "Adopt a Millennial Today!" by becoming a mentor. We've got so much to learn from each other. Emmy has taught me about technology and shared tools with me to make me more productive, more creative, and to give everything I do a more professional polish. In turn, I have taught her the value of good leadership and how to get along with all kinds of people in the workplace. I know what some of my baby boomer friends are thinking out there: "Hey, it took me a long time to get where I am today." And I appreciate that. But how does keeping all of that wisdom and knowledge to yourself help anyone? Grab a young mentee today and teach them what you know. They'll give you a new perspective and maybe teach you a thing or two!

And let's all show each other a little empathy, shall we? The world we live in today is a crazy place. We're all clinging to this planet together. I challenge you to put yourself in someone else's shoes and really understand their point of view without judgment and see what happens!

LYNNE HAYES has been an instructional designer, teacher and motivator for more than 20 years. Her preferred title as Learning Leader is only the beginning of her diverse resume. From leading national sales programs, increasing organizational collaboration, formulating better corporate communication styles and providing executive leadership coaching, Lynne has developed efficient and effective programs that last.

One of the first questions she'll ask is, "How can I help?" With a strong understanding of the changing workforce, she is an innovator when it comes to adapting traditional leadership styles with the unique challenges facing our modern workplace.

Lynne customizes leadership coaching, sales training, and communication workshops to fit every audience, from startup to Fortune 500 Company. Her professional interests include: millennials in the workplace, sales team motivation, and individual professional

continued

leadership coaching. With her dynamic mix of encouragement, tools, passion, and facts, she helps people add value to what they do every day.

When she is not traveling, Lynne loves to spend time playing ball with her rescue pup, Mabel; early morning runs and cycling classes; coffee with her husband John; and contributing motherly words of wisdom to group texts with her grown-up kids, Emmy and Sam.

Lynne Hayes

linkedin.com/in/workonwork

Redefining Success
Johnna Beckham

There are two things that have tested me more than I ever thought possible: being a single mother and being an entrepreneur. And while it might not seem like the two have anything to do with one another, I've learned they are more similar than I ever could have imagined.

My son Levi was eight years old when his father and I divorced. The first few years were incredibly difficult for the two of us taking the world on alone. Explaining to a child why his dad decided to leave us was painful, and finances were a constant worry. Discipline was perhaps the thing that threw me for the greatest loop. I had always envisioned—expected—a father to handle disciplining my child. I was ready to be the nurturing mother, but laying the hammer down wasn't something I was mentally prepared for.

We all expect to be successful at marriage—even though the odds certainly aren't in our favor—so when my marriage fell apart, I felt like a failure and saw a road of failure ahead. Nurturing my child and keeping our lives together...alone. People would look at me like my situation was broken. How could I raise this child without a father?

I had to reframe my definition of "success." Embracing that I was a failure wasn't going to get us anywhere good anytime soon.

I needed to set a strong example for my son. I couldn't fall apart—I had no choice. And so I redefined what success meant to me.

That meant having confidence to play many roles that I might not have if I weren't a single parent. Many times I became nurse, leader, mom, dad, teacher, and most importantly, empathetic disciplinarian. It taught me perseverance and creativity, especially since I had no idea what went through the brain of a teenage boy. Each role brought a new perspective on how to approach a situation with different tasks and initiatives.

Boundaries and goals had to be set in order to accomplish—or better yet, survive—each day. I found solutions that filled my gaps, I prioritized my family over myself for a long time, and I put myself out of my comfort zone to do things that I knew were good for my child but might not have been what I felt I was good at. Did I make mistakes? Of course I did. All of the time. But I also made major accomplishments, each bringing me more independence because I realized that I could be strong enough to overcome anything in spite of making mistakes.

I would learn a few years down the road, when I would one day become an entrepreneur, how much I would do all of those same things, but instead for my business.

As time has a tendency to do, it passed quickly, and before I knew it, Levi was leaving for college. He was ready to become an adult, and I had managed to help him get there.

To keep our finances stable and give me the flexibility of time to be both mom and dad, I had been working in corporate America throughout Levi's childhood. Although my position in the corporate world was necessary during those years, I always had an underlying yearning to stretch myself. When Levi graduated, that yearning for independence in my career became stronger. I felt that I'd given my life to being responsible for my son, but now it was time to be a little irresponsible and do something for myself. I didn't have the huge responsibility to be a single parent anymore, so I could take chances and risks. I made the decision to start school at the same time my son went off to college. I decided to get my MBA.

In 2013, I entered the Executive MBA program at Washington University in St. Louis. I wasn't quite sure what I was going to do with my MBA; if nothing else, it would be an accomplishment that would benefit my growth in my corporate job. But at the end of my education, the entrepreneurial bug bit me. I had an idea to create a line of custom suiting for women. I shared the idea with a professor, secured investment, and started a business: Johnna Marie.

I quickly learned that while I felt equipped for independence, I had convinced myself that freedom comes with ease. I was so wrong, and I was now knee-deep in a whole new parenting adventure! And I can't tell you how many times I have used lessons learned as a single parent in managing my own business.

Like parenting, I had so many people question whether I had the skills to do it. Did I 100 percent know what I was doing for managing finances, operations, marketing, and HR? Of course not!

But I figured it out. Just like with parenting and my struggles with discipline, finances, and caretaking, I found the resources I needed, I persevered, and I figured it out.

I also never realized how much a business is like a family. When I started hiring team members, they looked to me as the leader, and I had the responsibility to rise to that occasion. I couldn't just be their friend. Being the leader was much more similar to parenting than I ever imagined. Leaders and managers must discipline, encourage, guide, laugh, and cry with their team if they want their team members to be productive, motivated, satisfied, grow, and stay with the company.

Not surprisingly, discipline and guidance were some of the toughest managerial skills for me, just as they were in parenting. One woman who worked for me was terrific and talented...but not at the role she was in. She would make mistake after mistake, regardless of the corrective action and feedback I'd give. I was heartbroken and frustrated, but over time it became clear that this just wasn't the right position for her. Keeping her in that role meant she couldn't succeed, and she was being held back. By releasing her, I allowed her to go find a position that fit her skills. Today, she and I see each other regularly, and she thanked me for letting her go. She is succeeding, and isn't that just what we all want for ourselves, our children, and our team members?

Reframing what success means in parenting was transformational for me back then. As an entrepreneur, reframing what success means in business has been transformational for me now. As a cash-strapped small business owner, there have been many sleepless nights when I wondered whether checks would clear and whether I could finance payroll. But all of that stress and worry are silenced when I hear that my business has positively impacted someone's life.

Now, success is the fact that I've created a place where people can make a living and grow professionally. I make an impact on my customers' lives through my products. Even in the months where the bank balance was very small, that new perspective of success has helped me persevere.

In both parenting and entrepreneurism, there is a strong fear of failure. In both roles, I'm constantly hoping and praying that I'm doing it right...but you never really know if you are! I vividly remember having a conversation with a friend about his fear of becoming a parent. His fear of failure was so high. My advice to him was, "Be prepared to do it wrong, make mistakes, and forgive yourself for bad decisions. Kids are resilient."

Little did I know that same advice would ring in my ears daily when owning a business. There aren't enough books, friends, or family members that can explain the tests you will encounter. There are no quick fixes. There is nothing that can help you be certain of the decisions you're making.

I'm now several years into the role of an entrepreneur. It's not any easier now than it was when I first started, but I have learned a lot, and I've actually grown as a parent through the process too.

I genuinely believe that had I not misstepped in my life and career, I wouldn't have grown as a parent or leader. Lessons would have been missed.

As difficult as those early years of single parenthood felt at the time, I cherish them. Levi and I taught each other what it meant to be independent and resilient. To laugh when you feel like crying and to know you are always a work in progress. Always growing.

I never expected business ownership to be so similar to raising a child. But in both cases, nothing is more exciting than when you see your people grow and become leaders themselves. I've learned to measure my success by the people who depend on me. And I have to say, we're all doing pretty well right now.

JOHNNA BECKHAM is the founder and CEO of both Johnna Marie and BOOST Apparel Group. Johnna has more than 20 years of business management, sales, and marketing experience, and has held key positions within Fortune 500 companies with increasing leadership roles. During two decades of working in corporate America, Johnna noticed a problem she shared with many female colleagues: the inability to find suits that fit and flatter a woman's body. While on residency with the Executive MBA program at Washington University, an idea was created to form a business that solves that problem by offering custom made clothing for women. Along with Ron King, Johnna has taken the business from the basement of her home to an office and manufacturing space located on South Vandeventer Avenue in St Louis.

Johnna Beckham

jbeckham@boostapparelgroup.com

boostapparelgroup.com | facebook.com/boostapparelgroup

linkedin.com/in/johnnabeckham | instagram.com/boostapparelgroup

ᗺ

How Did I Get Here?

Julie Jones

"...and you may find yourself in another part of the world...and you may ask yourself, well, how did I get here?" – Talking Heads

So there we were: the only two Caucasians in a French bakery located in downtown Seoul, South Korea, packed with a sea of early-morning commuters patiently waiting for their morning coffee. We sat at our small bistro table, nervously picking at a croissant as we waited for our lives to change forever.

It was August 2, 2010, which just so happened to be our 13th wedding anniversary. As we watched the minutes tick by, it was impossible not to wonder whether we should just turn around and go back to the beautiful life we had built together over the past 13 years. Were we sure about this decision?

At that same moment in an adoption center next door, two kind, generous, and loving individuals were holding tight to a one-year-old boy they had raised since he was just two days old. As foster parents, this couple had taken great care of this little boy's needs, preparing him for the massive change about to take place in his life. Saying goodbye to this boy who was about to move to the other side of the world was extremely difficult for this family, whose sadness was eased only by the happiness they felt for his future. Unlike so many other children, this boy's forever family had found him and were waiting next door in a French bakery to meet him.

The adoption process was a very fast few months of shuffling paperwork, sitting through interviews, and preparing our family and home for our son. In the stillness at our table that morning, I looked at Billy and asked him, "Are we making the right choice for our family?" There would be no turning back.

Together, we heard ourselves say aloud, "Yes." We had faith in God that we were making the right decision, not only for this baby, but for our two older boys, too. We paid our bill, walked into the door of the adoption center, and into our new life as Teddy's parents.

We spent an emotional morning with Teddy and his foster parents. We immediately fell in love with this beautiful child and knew at that moment our family was complete.

Sometimes, the most meaningful, rewarding, and beautiful decisions in life require a leap of faith; to walk through a door and never look back. We thank God daily for blessing us with Teddy. We are so proud to be his parents. Teddy has made our family complete, our lives more meaningful, and our faith stronger. Little did I know that making that most important leap of faith for our family would be the first in a series of decisions that have fundamentally transformed my career and my life.

The year prior, I turned 40. There's something about milestone birthdays that lead us to stop and reflect. I loved my family and my life. As I blew out my candles, however, I realized that life is too short. I really started to consider what makes me happy, what doesn't make me happy, and what I can do to live life to the fullest.

I realized that my dreams and pursuits have always catered to society's expectations. I needed to step outside my comfort zone.

Like many of us, I spent the first 20 years of adulthood on autopilot: working hard, pursuing my dreams, and achieving success in my education and career. I lucked out by marrying an amazing man who loves and supports me, and we had two incredible boys, Will and Henry. Being their mom has always brought so much joy to my life, and they continue to be the center of my world. I realized I didn't want to change my life; I wanted to be proactive and create more for my life.

For most of those 20 years, I was a practicing attorney and had what looked like nothing short of a happy career on paper. I had great mentors and supportive bosses and liked working with and learning from my colleagues. But deep down, I can't say I ever fully enjoyed the practice of law. I couldn't wait to get home to my kids after work, and I really had a hard time finding balance in my life.

When my oldest son started kindergarten, I decided to leave my law career and become a stay-at-home mom. And I loved it...for the first few years. But when I found myself face-to-face with those 40 birthday candles and those "life is too short" thoughts, it gave me a new sense of bravery to look inside myself and my life to discover what was missing.

One year later, we brought our son, Teddy, home from South Korea. He was one of the pieces that had been missing.

My family was complete, but my career was not. After the success of growing our family, I realized I was ready to continue stepping forward. I didn't love practicing law, but I did love traveling the world and exploring new territory, unchartered by me. Somehow, I was going to figure out how to turn my love of travel into a career.

And so in August 2013, three years after we adopted Teddy, I found myself standing outside the entryway to the Bellagio Hotel in Las Vegas on an extremely hot day. Inside those doors was the Virtuoso Travel Week conference where luxury hoteliers, cruise lines, and tour companies network with luxury travel advisors with the shared goal of creating new, exciting experiences for travelers around the world. More than 4,000 people from 58 countries had arrived in Vegas for this networking extravaganza. Earlier that year, I had started my travel agency, TopFlight Travels. I traveled to Vegas to network and make my first connections and friendships in the industry. I didn't know a single person inside that building. "How on Earth did I get here?" I asked myself.

I jumped into the travel industry and faced the unknown. While I was certainly confident in my ability to create amazing travel experiences down to the last detail, which I had been doing personally for years, parlaying that passion into a successful career included many challenges. Without a mentor or guide, I taught myself the business, from how to make a simple hotel booking to organizing a complex, month-long, customized tour of Europe. I also taught myself the basics of owning a business with much trial and error, such as how to market my business, work with accountants, create my own website, find the right assistant, learn how to effectively delegate to that assistant, manage a budget and expenditures....the list goes on and on. It has been nice saving money by serving as my own attorney.

After a few years, things got serious. To take my business to the next level, I needed to make connections with industry leaders so I could learn from their success. Aligning my company with Brownell Travel has been a huge part of that growth. As part of this tribe, I now have the support and guidance that were previously missing. Each day brings new challenges, new learning opportunities, and long hours, and each day I forget that I have a job. I am so grateful to have made my passion for travel into a successful career.

Getting to this place in my career has required me to step out of my comfort zone on many occasions, take chances, have faith that all will work out at the end of the day, and allow myself to make mistakes and learn from them. The experience of adopting Teddy has taught me that I can be brave and take risks. Without that experience, I may not have taken the leap into the travel industry.

While learning to be a travel advisor with no guidance took some smarts, I am grateful I'm smart enough to know there is so much about the industry that I do not know. Brownell has really filled that need for professional guidance. Tui Leatherman, a lifelong friend and travel advisor for TopFlight Travels, has also been a fantastic wingman, supporting me whenever things get tough. Similarly, RISE Collaborative fills my need for community support. I am able to surround myself with other women who motivate, inspire, and provide me with incredible examples of successful women in our St. Louis community.

How did I get here? I took a leap of faith and walked through the door. The door to the adoption agency, the door to the Bellagio Hotel, the door to my true self. I got here by stepping out of my comfort zone and bravely facing the unknown full steam ahead with hard work, grit, and by surrounding myself with the right people.

Now when I find myself sipping a coffee at a French café, I get to call it "work," and there are no nerves, because I've never been more alive and comfortable in my own skin. I am supported and fulfilled. I am authentically me.

JULIE JONES is the Founder and President of TopFlight Travels, a new-generation travel agency that plans, executes, and delivers extraordinary travel experiences for its clients. TopFlight Travels utilizes a unique discovery process that captures what will make every client's trip unique and special. Every detail is handled by Julie's team, allowing for hassle-free travel. When not planning trips of a lifetime for her clients, Julie travels to new destinations to research hotels, resorts, and tours so that her expertise can better serve her clients. Julie previously practiced commercial finance law at Bryan Cave and is a graduate of Mary Institute, Boston College, and St. Louis University School of Law. Julie lives in St. Louis with her husband and three darling boys.

Julie Jones

julie@topflighttravels.com

topflighttravels.comfac | ebook.com/topflighttravels | instagram.com/topflighttravels

B

Stay Safe
Jessica Rask

When I was 15, my mom said to me, "Jessica, you must always be sure you can take care of yourself." That singular, empowering statement has resonated with me everyday since, encouraging my independence at a formative age. It also pushed me to make decisions regarding my educational and career path that may appear risky to others who prefer a road more commonly traveled.

Playing it safe has never suited me.

When faced with choices, I always tended to choose the less traveled path just to see what was around the corner. Often, my decisions were met with comments from well-meaning others telling me, "You can't do that," or, "Are you sure that's a good idea?" Everyone wanted to protect me from undue difficulty or help me make practical decisions, but I usually found the more difficult route led me to awfully interesting places.

By all accounts, I should have led a fairly "safe" life. Raised in a blue collar, middle class, Catholic family in the middle of the United States, my parents taught the seven of us to be practical with our time and our money.

I studied Latin in high school to boost my vocabulary for the SAT. One day, our teacher announced she would organize a

Spring Break trip to two places where Latin is literally carved on the walls: Greece and Italy. I begged my parents and they agreed that if I earned half of the cost, I could go. Immediately, I applied for a second job and started saving. Six months later, I landed in Athens with Mrs. Horgan and others from school.

I loved every moment of that trip, including the surprise of seeing soldiers with machine guns standing guard as we exited the plane, which was normal in this foreign land. Culture shock! I toured the Acropolis and stood in wonder at a sight so ancient. I soaked in the white buildings contrasting against the deep, blue of the ocean and sky. I welcomed the challenge of communicating through more than words. The food tasted better, the markets sounded more boisterous, the people appeared livelier.

We took an overnight ferry to Italy where I saw even more glorious, new things. Incredible food, of course! Ancient ruins everywhere. Motorbikes speeding past me. A glamour I'd never witnessed before. I felt free and alive on that trip abroad, perhaps more so than ever before. It sparked a thirst that could only be quenched by seeking out more.

The trip turned out to be my first of many times abroad. Before I graduated college, I would go on to visit seven more countries, each trip financed by me.

The excitement of a broader world inspired my decision to go away for college. Family and friends asked why I would turn down scholarship money to quality in-state universities. They wondered why I'd want to leave the supportive community of home.

I decided to attend The University of Michigan. Public, enormous, far from home, co-ed, and secular – it was everything my Catholic school education was not. And that was everything.

Education is generated as much from experiences and interactions as from books, and my views were challenged the moment my parents dropped me at my dorm. I made friends from all over the country and world, and for the first time engaged with people who were Jewish, Hindu, Muslim, Protestant, and Atheist. It was as if I had been walking through a forest of the same familiar scenery up to this point, when the trees opened up to a much broader field. By leaving my "safe" home, I was able to take in an entire world of opinions and mindsets that had been distant to me. In many ways, it felt no different than stepping off of that first airplane in Athens.

Taking the adventurous route to an out of state college had left me with a mountain of student loans, so after graduation I made an uncharacteristically "safe" choice and took a job with Ernst & Young. The salary and benefits were great, things were stable, and there were opportunities to travel abroad on the company's dime! I requested a transfer abroad and less than three months later, I was packing my bags for Amsterdam to work with colleagues from around the globe.

I made the most of my time there, actively going out of my comfort zone to befriend Dutch people rather than spending all of my time with other Americans from work. I taught myself to ride a bicycle like the locals, learned to speak Dutch, and made friends who embraced me like family. I spent holidays with their families, traveled with them, and learned everything I could about their culture. They helped me to feel at home in another country and culture in a way I never expected.

When Ernst & Young requested I return to the United States after two years in the Netherlands, I declined and instead stayed in Amsterdam with a boutique, Dutch consulting firm.

"You're crazy!" people said. "What if something happens at home? What if you get cancer?!?"

Instead of the human resources department of a major corporation organizing my visas, permits, taxes, healthcare, and housing, it was now all up to me and I learned to navigate whatever came my way.

After two years with the Dutch firm, I took another leap of faith to follow a passion. Yoga had gone from an occasional form of exercise to something that I wanted to live and breathe. I had seen how the practice had impacted my health, mental wellbeing, and outlook, and I wanted to spread that to others. I left my consulting job to teach yoga full time, and it was immediately clear this was not a popular decision among those closest to me.

"Why would you leave such a lucrative career to make almost no money teaching yoga? You worked so hard to get through business school! It's not wise!"

Without vision of what the future would hold, it surely seemed as though I was throwing my career to the wayside to pursue what others say as little more than a hobby.

After a year of teaching, I still craved more of a challenge than showing up to lead a class every day. After five years abroad, I was finally ready to return to the US to be closer to family.

Combining my passion for teaching yoga with my business background, I built two yoga schools in Chicago and St. Louis. Six-figures worth of loans and my life's savings brought the schools to life. Always one to seek out new opportunities, I also opened a cold-pressed juicery called St. Louis Juice Press inside my St. Louis yoga school. Why not? I had a captive audience and St. Louis was lacking in cold-pressed juice; I recognized the business opportunity and took it.

It would be deceptive to act as though my career changes and lifestyle choices were easy. In Amsterdam, I went from fancy living in a swanky apartment during my consulting days to living in a studio with nothing more than a futon and some clothes. I missed some significant family events while living abroad that left me feeling alienated, lonely, and even triggered bouts of depression.

Building and running the two yoga schools 300 miles away from each other was a strain – financially and physically. I found my own health and wellness suffered while I tried to give of myself to others. To better care for myself, I sold my Chicago yoga school in 2013. Right after I opened the St. Louis Juice Press, the city went through a major period of unrest. The business district where both my yoga school and my juice bar were located took a direct hit and my fellow small business owners and I were forced to board up for a week at a crucial time in my business cycle. I almost filed for bankruptcy and waitressed on nights and weekends to keep both of the businesses afloat.

After two and a half years of burning my candle at both ends, I closed the doors to my St. Louis yoga school and sold the Juice Press 18 months later. I'm back in consulting now, but on my own terms, and have so many experiences to draw on when advising my clients because of my own business ventures.

The winding road has challenged and humbled me, broken me down, and built me back up. It has encouraged me to remain open-minded and enabled me to find a partner in life who would never ask me to be anything less than exactly who I am, even if that changes day to day. With every decision and every different path, I met incredible people, learned, grew, and shaped my worldview in a way that is totally different than I could have ever imagined before I headed to Greece, Ann Arbor, or Amsterdam.

We never know what tomorrow has in store for us. All along the way I have been asked, "Why?" The better question is, "Why not?" To quote my yoga mentor, I now know the only answer is and always has been, "Because I can."

My advice: trust your instincts, take risks, and navigate your own future rather than allowing others to do it for you. I know that I will always be safe on my own and able to take care of myself, just as my mom's advice empowered me to so long ago. If you consider safety to be adventure, join my team.

JESSICA RASK acts as Chief Operating Officer and as a Director in the Transfer Pricing and Valuation Services practice of WTP Advisors; an independent firm specialized in international tax, export incentives (IC-Disc), transfer pricing, valuation, and tax process innovation solutions. Jessica graduated from the University of Michigan Ross School of Business and holds the Certified Valuation Analyst (CVA) credential from the National Association of Certified Valuators and Analysts. Jessica began her career with Ernst & Young and lived in Amsterdam, the Netherlands, for five years where she assisted multinational clients in a wide range of industries, as well as taught a course for the International Bureau of Fiscal Documentation's International Tax Academy.

In 2012, Jessica participated in Goldman Sachs' 10,000 Small Business Initiative and was voted "Most Likely to Franchise" by her peers. Prior to joining WTP Advisors, Jessica founded two businesses:

Hot Yoga Midwest, with locations in Chicago and St. Louis, and the St. Louis Juice Press in St. Louis. When she's not assisting her clients with transfer pricing and/or business valuation issues, Jessica can be found spending time with her family, reading historical fiction, practicing yoga, assisting the homeless, advocating for refugee communities, and of course, traveling.

Jessica Rask

jessica.rask@wtpadvisors.com

wtpadvisors.com | linkedin.com/in/jessica-rask

Making the Call
Kate Kerr

Nine years ago, I had a call to make. I felt ill. My mouth was dry and my stomach felt like it was filled with rocks. Feelings of doubt, anxiety, and concern swirled around my mind. I was sitting on a couch in a small San Francisco apartment preparing to make a call that would change my career and future forever.

Was I making the right decision? I wasn't certain. Would I be able to rebuild my career after making this call? Probably, but I didn't know how.

In the call, I planned to reject a job offer that had already cost me 10 years of my life and tens of thousands of dollars in education. It wasn't a decision I took lightly.

I was at a career crossroads. I had an offer for a dream job in the foreign service of the United States Agency for International Development (USAID) in a role that focused on regulatory and development initiatives. The job would take me around the world and allow me to live in several different countries, each for two to three years. Given my love of travel and focus in international development, I couldn't believe the U.S. Government was going to pay me to live that life! I felt like I'd won the lottery. The interview process had been intense and included tests, several interviews, dozens of essays, and a lengthy background check.

Leading up to this moment, I'd spent years working in jobs designed to give me the skills, knowledge, experience, and financial resources to prepare me for the role. After college, I spent three years in strategy consulting, including a year working in Guatemala with a women's co-op to help build their business and drive revenue. After graduating from law school, I worked in a global law firm, where I gained a sophisticated set of tools to navigate the world and learn how to be effective in the pursuit of justice and development. I spent a year in India on a Fulbright studying the ramifications of the legal system and the development roadblocks facing those vulnerable to forced labor.

After all the efforts and investment, how could I give up this offer?

I hadn't accounted for meeting someone who would give me second thoughts about the path I was pursuing...my husband.

Before you assume I was swept off my feet and threw away my career for romantic whimsy, let me assure you that's not what happened. While some say the story of our first date sounds like a romantic comedy (another story for another day), I wasn't looking for happily ever after in the love department. I've been an "I am woman, hear me roar" type of lady since high school and never considered myself a romantic.

When I received my orientation date for USAID, my now-husband asked me not to go. It wasn't an "either/or" situation. It was a, "Would you consider staying so that we could live in the same country?" kind of question.

I was conflicted.

I spent the next month engaging in reflection about how I wanted to spend my life and focused my decision around answering four key questions:

What did I want to achieve?

Why did I want to achieve it?

How would I achieve it?

What was I willing to sacrifice?

What did I want to achieve? For the preceding 10 years, I thought I wanted a life of adventure. I wanted that adventure to be focused on building more opportunity and equality for others. After consideration, I found my answer to be vague, limited, and self-serving.

I was stumped. When I was young I remembered wanting big jobs that had big impact. I wanted to be the President of the United States. I wanted to work at the U.N. I wanted to run a major global corporation. Instead of big, my career goal seemed to be focused on what was practical and possible. I was uneasy about my conclusion but continued with the process, promising myself I'd return to this question.

Why did I want to achieve it? If my goal was to find a job that took me abroad but also was engaging and impactful, I needed to answer why I wanted to achieve this goal by knowing me better. I reflected on my strengths, values, and motivations.

I talked to family members and friends, former colleagues and mentors. I shared stories about times at work when I'd excelled and when I'd struggled and the moments I'd most enjoyed. I looked at tasks I'd avoided and experiences I'd rather forget. I stared at the things that scared me. In this reflection, I found natural strengths and uncovered values.

I came to see that my strengths included curiosity and adaptability (I could easily transition to different cultures, countries, and industries). I could strategize and was at my best when it came to building programs, projects, and structure.

I recognized that I was motivated by the opportunity to bring positive change to others. I wanted to spend my time building structures and systems that improved lives. Taking the time to understand why I was interested in the job helped me think about how I might achieve my actual goal beyond this job.

How would I achieve it? I needed to better understand my options. I called everyone I knew at USAID. I peppered them with questions about their day-to-day highs and lows, the job's impact on family and relationships, and the advancement options. I learned that while the tasks were interesting, there were frustrations, as there are in every job.

Perhaps the USAID job would satisfy my why, but I started to realize it wasn't the only one that would play to my strengths or satisfy my values. I also considered the struggle of a long-distance relationship and what it meant to live abroad and start a family. Pulling the thoughts together, I saw the how may not need to be a singular track or job. Perhaps there were other paths that satisfied the how.

What was I willing to sacrifice? I grew up foregoing sleep, time with friends, and creature comforts to excel in school and to pursue opportunities in international development. Those sacrifices didn't feel like sacrifices to me at the time, but I wasn't certain I'd feel the same for the rest of my life. Did I want to be a career nomad forever?

Ultimately, I made the call that changed my life. I gave up the dream job at USAID because, after examining my goals and values, I believed I'd be able to find a different job that gave me the platform to draw on my strengths, offer enough flexibility to stretch my curiosity, and provide an avenue to make a positive impact on the lives of others. I believed I'd be able to still see the world in a way that didn't feel like a sacrifice to other interests.

After that call, I took weeks to reflect on my career crossroads. I spent two more years with a nagging sense of self-doubt and insecurity about my decision. I found peace when I took the time to return to the beginning of the process to define what I wanted to achieve. I didn't want to set my sights on a goal that would only be interesting and attainable. I wanted something more—something that would leverage my strengths and values but was not limited by them. I committed to crafting a vision that would be big and allow for bold goals.

My vision offers me an image of my future life. I may not know how to reach that future, but it guides how I spend time and energy, set goals, and choose roles. It's focused around helping others build engaging and satisfying careers on an individual and organizational level. So in my current role, I wear two hats: one in recruiting and one in professional development. With my recruiting hat, I talk to others about their career history. With my professional development hat, I work on building structures and platforms for career development.

In my daily study of career choices and insights, I've come to realize that the what, why, and how in the career decision making process also needs to be informed by self-awareness, perceptiveness and knowledge of the market and opportunities. These reflection points enable smart career moves. They allow you to intentionally see the opportunity in front of you, be engaged, find meaning, and align efforts. While I followed sound logic to make a very difficult decision, it didn't make that call turning down the USAID job any easier to make. But it got me right where I need to be and I'm grateful for it. Helping others forge their path is my vision and I'm living it out each day. And that's a pretty good place to be.

KATE KERR is a career development professional. As a former Big Law attorney, Big 4 strategy consulting analyst, Fulbright Scholar, and nonprofit leader, Kate has experience in career development and transitions.

In her current role as the Director of Recruiting and Professional Development at Armstrong Teasdale LLP, Kate focuses on finding talented people and helping them build great careers. She has been instrumental in the creation and development of the AT Leadership Institute, diverse learning systems, and talent development programs at the law firm.

She holds a JD cum laude from Georgetown University Law Center, a BA with honors from Grinnell College, a Fulbright, and the SHRM-SCP certification. She serves as a board member for the Women's

Foundation of Greater St. Louis and sits on the Advisory Board for RISE Society.

Outside of work, Kate married the man in the story and they share a son together. She also enjoys writing, presenting, and facilitating programs focused on developing your better professional self. Connect with her on LinkedIn to continue the conversation around careers.

Kate Kerr

katekerrcareers@gmail.com

linkedin.com/in/kate-kerr

In This Moment
Kate Wiegmann

February 7, 2017

My business partner, Stacy, and I stood at the doors of our business, RISE Collaborative, as the first guests to our grand opening arrived. We looked at each other and smiled.

"We really did this!" we said to each other with our eyes in the unspoken language that only comes with working side-by-side and one-on-one through the time, stress, and excitement of building a company.

We had poured ourselves into this idea and company, and this was the celebration and official launch of all of our hard work. We knew, of course, the hard work would continue, but we embraced that next chapter with open arms. Hard work, creativity, and working as long and hard as it took to reach our sky-high dreams was part of who we were and how we got to this point.

In that moment, we were partners, entrepreneurs, and friends.

May 30, 2017

And so there I was, walking through the aisles of Target, when my phone rang and my life changed.

"It worked," the woman's voice on the other end of the line said. I stopped moving. I stopped breathing. My heart fluttered.

"Are you sure?" I asked. "I thought it was too early."

"I've been doing this a long time and I'm 100-percent sure," she said. "You are pregnant!"

Happy I most certainly was, but also nervous, excited, and a little afraid. It had been a long wait for this pregnancy, and my husband and I had experienced loss along that bumpy road. Part of me wondered all along whether that pain was a sign motherhood wasn't my path. That the energy, time, and joy of growing our business, which had served as a helpful and convenient distraction during the past painful year, was my real baby.

We'd used fertility treatments to conceive, so our doctor knew the exact date of conception (romantic, I know…!) When he told me the estimated due date, I couldn't help but laugh: February 7, the same date as our grand opening anniversary.

Maybe this was a sign after all—that this baby would be intrinsically tied to my "business baby" with the same birthday! That this pregnancy would be healthy, and I was meant to have both the baby and the business.

Stacy was overjoyed at the news and as a self-proclaimed "math nerd," especially the dates.

In that moment, I was an optimist and, apparently, a mother.

September 10, 2017

Both of our families were coming to our house for a gender reveal party. A little narcissistic? Maybe. But we were at the halfway point in our pregnancy and figured any excuse to celebrate how uneventful things had been so far was reason enough. When you've come from bad news, no news is very good news!

Because the pregnancy had been so easy—no nausea, acne, or fatigue—all of the old wives' tales told us there was a boy in there. As a woman business owner whose business is focused on supporting and strengthening women and who is surrounded by women all day every day, I knew I was going to raise this young man a little differently. He would only see women doctors, would always think of women as his equals, and would play golf instead of football! I was going to raise a modern man.

When the pink confetti flew around our heads, I was stunned. Thrilled, really. I realized in that moment how much I had really wanted to have a little girl. My work and the incredible power of women had reshaped what I thought of myself and how I thought about the future of women. I was empowered and excited to raise a smart, strong, successful little GIRL.

I texted Stacy a photo of the pink confetti scattered around our backyard, and she replied, "I KNEW IT! How could you NOT have a little girl?!"

In that moment, I was a feminist and...the most shocked person on the planet.

December 22, 2017

I was a mess. As per usual right before the holidays, an entire year's worth of work needed to be accomplished before the year closed out. I was completely behind on my Christmas shopping and had shouted at my husband more times than I care to admit. My mind was a million places and it was showing at work.

Who was I kidding? The baby wasn't even here and I couldn't keep it together! I was failing at work and at life. I was letting Stacy down, letting our members down, and really letting myself down. Did I have incredibly high standards and a serious case of perfectionism? Yes. But did recognizing that mean I felt any less like a failure? No, it did not.

In this moment, I was overwhelmed, defeated, and...looking for a time travel machine.

January 21, 2018

The day before, Stacy texted me saying she dreamt I went into labor, to which I responded with that hysterical laughter emoji and the comment, "Yeah, wouldn't that just be our luck?!" Our first full-time employee had just started, we were scrambling to get our first book to the printer, and our one year anniversary party was just around the corner. This baby couldn't come yet.

But then she did. Romy June Wiegmann arrived early, which she didn't yet realize is uncharacteristic for her parents! And there was no appropriate emoji to accompany the text to Stacy that morning to tell her that her dream was, in fact, a premonition. She was, of course, thrilled beyond measure and hid any fear and frustration from me.

It's true: newborn babies are every bit as terrifying and helpless as promised, and my husband and I were every bit as terrified and exhausted as promised, but in this strangely beautiful way. She trusted us to care for her, and we rose to the occasion. And part of that, I later realized, meant completely disconnecting from work for the first time in decades. It was strange and yet exactly where I needed to be.

In that moment, we became parents.

February 7, 2018

Through tears, laughter, and a lot of input from Google, we figured out the early days of parenting. When my husband returned to work, the days were lonely and scary. The revolving door of family and friends coming to meet the baby and bring us food stopped turning, and it was up to me to keep her fed, clean, rested, entertained, and physically and mentally stimulated for 10-plus hours. I never thought parenting would come naturally—

and goodness knows it didn't—but I honestly surprised myself at how I found strength, pride, and a new identity in this new world.

When I realized the date, I texted Stacy to wish her good luck at the anniversary party I was missing and how much I wished I could be there. But I was not prepared for the response. Text after text came through saying how much I was missed, not just by Stacy, but by our members, investors, and team members.

My heart ached to be there! For the first time in weeks, I remembered and missed the world outside of my home. And over the coming 10 weeks of my maternity leave, I would grapple with the balance between yearning to be at work while desperately loving this new world called Motherhood.

In this moment, I was torn but fulfilled.

April 17, 2018

I returned to work at RISE Collaborative with anxiety, anticipation, and apprehension. I missed Romy. I missed my old self. I loved the stimulating conversation of the workplace and getting to approach challenges that I actually felt I could tackle. But I simultaneously missed those quiet, tender days with my girl, making up ridiculous lullabies for her and the pride I felt when they made her smile.

The days, weeks, and months that followed were filled with successes and failures at home and at work. Missed deadlines and miscommunications with Stacy and my husband. Growth and laughter from our baby and at work. But somehow, the negatives about yourself always seem to carry more weight than the positives.

I found myself lost in this grey area not knowing how to define myself. I definitely felt like a mother now, but how did that balance with the business owner role? If I felt I was failing so badly at these roles, how could I possibly embrace them? Wouldn't it be easier—better—for everyone if I just picked one and focused on that? Maybe then I could do that one *pretty well* rather than trying to fake it through two.

How fortunate I am to work in a place filled with other women who have walked this path before. Who are walking it with me. Who are trying to decide if they want to walk it one day, too. It's through this community, an incredibly sensitive business partner, and a supportive husband that I'm learning to push that negative and defeating self talk aside and to embrace all of my new roles. I'm doing it imperfectly, while filled with plenty of self doubt, apprehension, and awareness of how things have changed, but I've come to appreciate how I've grown through this as a friend, partner, and professional.

In this moment, I am empowered. I'm open to all of the lessons life will bring my way through the classrooms of parenthood, entrepreneurship, and marriage. And while part of me hopes my daughter never has these same struggles with self-doubt, identity, and acceptance, I also know that discomfort is part of the journey to a full and happy life. So instead I'll set as good of an example as I can and stand beside her as she walks her path, wherever it may lead her.

KATE WIEGMANN is Chief Operating Officer of RISE Collaborative Workspace, a female-focused business community that provides coworking space and resources to help its members find success both personally and professionally. Prior to opening RISE Collaborative, Kate worked in public relations and marketing representing large national brands as well as local businesses, nonprofits, and politicians in her second home of Greenville, South Carolina. A graduate of the University of Missouri School of Journalism, Kate is a skilled storyteller and writer. When she's not passionately supporting St. Louis businesswomen and growing her startup company, she is a freelance writer, consults in interior design, and volunteers with Big Brothers Big Sisters and St. Louis Children's Hospital.

Kate Wiegmann

kate@riseworkspace.com

RISEworkspace.com | facebook.com/RISECollaborativeWorkspace | twitter.com/RISEcollabwkspc
instagram.com/RISECollaborativeWorkspace | linkedin.com/in/kate-wiegmann

Afterword
Abby Mros

We started this anthology reflecting on community, connections, and confidence. I was lucky enough to join the RISE St. Louis team in the summer of 2018, and I can easily say that we live by these three things every day. I love working in a space where these three aspects are so deeply held and practiced.

I received my MSW from the Brown School of Social Work at Washington University in St. Louis. I am passionate about supporting survivors of gender-based violence and am currently under supervision for my clinical license. I know firsthand how important community, connections, and confidence are, both for myself and for my clients. Before my MSW, I received my B.A. from WashU in Psychology and Women, Gender, & Sexuality Studies. Supporting and bolstering women has always been at the heart of who I am.

When we feel isolated, disconnected, or unconfident, we inherently feel worse. We don't want to reach out to our support systems, and we don't feel valuable. This is such a painful space to live in. But it's a common space, and sometimes a default space, if we don't intentionally try to counteract it. If instead we reach out, share ourselves with others, and find empowerment, we feel stronger and more fulfilled. And this is the work that is done at RISE.

We all see it every day in our St. Louis space and can especially feel it in the pages of this anthology.

I am so proud of the work, vulnerability, and strength that these authors put into their chapters. I hope that their words resonated with you, spoke to parts of you, and led you to make discoveries about your own life. That is the point of the work RISE does to empower women. And we luckily aren't stopping with just St. Louis. In 2019, RISE Denver will officially open its doors.

After that, the plan is to keep going and going. RISE Collaborative will continue to grow and continue to support women across the country and maybe even abroad. We know that there's so much more to learn in expanding this community, and we're going to do it through the power of connection and with a bit of blind confidence.

I hope that this anthology series will soon combine authors from all RISE Collaborative locations. Wouldn't it be amazing to open up this book and find women from all across the country recounting their stories of success and triumph? And knowing that the women in those pages all forged deeper connections with one another just from sharing and being vulnerable? I know I'm excited for that growth. That is what's at the heart of my work as a social worker, and it's at the heart of what I do at RISE, too. Thank you for being here with us for this second volume. We can't wait to see you again for Volume 3!

ABBY MROS graduated from Washington University in St. Louis in 2016 with a BA in Psychological & Brain Sciences and Women, Gender, & Sexuality Studies (WGSS). While at WashU she was heavily involved with university and student theatre. Abby entered the Brown School at WashU in Fall 2016 to pursue her Master's of Social Work. Abby's passion for WGSS led her to concentrate in Violence and Injury Prevention with women and specialize in Sexual Health and Education. She developed an expertise in the field of sex trafficking and commercial sexual exploitation, with specific consideration for systemtic and identity-based oppression.

After graduating in May 2018, Abby passed her first licensure exam and is now a Licensed Master Social Worker (LMSW) working on her clinical license (LCSW). Abby works part-time at Bridgeway Behavioral Health's Sexual Assault Center (SAC) as both a Sexual Assault Therapist and Youth Therapist. She provides trauma therapy, including evidence based treatments for PTSD, to

continued

adults and children/adolescents with experiences of sexual assault or intimate partner violence. Abby additionally works part-time at RISE Collaborative St. Louis on Communications & Programming, putting her analytical and organizational skills to work. Abby loves being part of the female-focused community at RISE and connecting with women in a wide variety of fields. She can't wait to see how this community grows!

Abby Mros

mros.abigail@gmail.com

linkedin.com/in/abby-mros

ᘔ